W9-AHR-823

PRACTICE MAKES PERFECT

English Vocabulary for Beginning ESL Learners

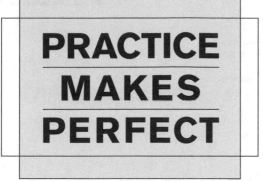

PRACTICE MAKES PERFECT

English Vocabulary for Beginning ESL Learners

Jean Yates

McGraw·Hill

New York   Chicago   San Francisco   Lisbon   London   Madrid   Mexico City
Milan   New Delhi   San Juan   Seoul   Singapore   Sydney   Toronto

The McGraw·Hill Companies

Copyright © 2006 by The McGraw-Hill Companies, Inc. All rights reserved. Printed in the
United States of America. Except as permitted under the United States Copyright Act of
1976, no part of this publication may be reproduced or distributed in any form or by any
means, or stored in a database or retrieval system, without the prior written permission of
the publisher.

6 7 8 9 0 QWD/QWD 0 9

ISBN-13: 978-0-07-146085-9
ISBN-10:   0-07-146085-3
Library of Congress Control Number: 2005933997

McGraw-Hill books are available at special quantity discounts to use as premiums and
sales promotions, or for use in corporate training programs. For more information, please
write to the Director of Special Sales, Professional Publishing, McGraw-Hill, Two Penn
Plaza, New York, NY 10121-2298. Or contact your local bookstore.

This book is printed on acid-free paper.

Contents

Introduction   viii

How to Use This Book   ix

PART I	Nouns	1

Unit 1   **People and Places**   3
Words for People   3
Words for Places   7

Unit 2   **Singular, Plural, and Noncount Nouns**   12
Using Singular Nouns   12
Using Plural Nouns   15
Using Noncount Nouns   22
Using Articles with Singular, Plural, and Noncount Nouns   28
Using Demonstrative Pronouns with Singular, Plural, and
      Noncount Nouns   31

Unit 3   **Proper Nouns**   33

Unit 4   **Possessive Nouns and Pronouns**   35
Possessive Nouns   35
Possessive Pronouns   36

Unit 5   **Review of Singular, Plural, and Noncount Nouns**   38

Unit 6   **Verbs Used as Nouns**   42

Unit 7   **More Specific Nouns**   44
Words for People   44
Words for the Arts   50
Words for Places   51
Words for Things   54
Words for Events   58

PART II   Adjectives   63

Unit 8   **Making Descriptions**   65
Adjectives That Describe People   65
Adjectives That Describe a Person's Condition   73
Adjectives That Describe Objects   76
Adjectives That Describe Places   80
Adjectives That Describe the Weather   81

Unit 9   **Comparisons and Superlatives**   83
Making an Adjective Stronger or Weaker   83
Making Comparisons with Adjectives   85
Expressing Superlatives   93

Unit 10   **Verbs and Nouns Used as Adjectives**   96
Verbs Used as Adjectives   96
Nouns Used as Adjectives   99

Unit 11   **Adjective Order**   104

PART III   Verbs   107

Unit 12   **The Verb *Be***   109
The Present Tense of *Be*   109
Asking Questions with *Be*   110
Making *Be* Negative   111
The Past Tense of *Be*   111

Unit 13   **Non–*To Be* Verbs**   113
Regular Present Tense Forms of Verbs Other than *Be*   113
Regular Past Tense Forms   115
Verbs That Describe Usual Activities   117
Irregular Past Tense Forms   119
Verbs Used for Household Activities   120
Verbs Used in a Classroom   123
Making Verbs Negative   124
Activities That Are Often Performed in an Office   126
Asking Questions   127
Verbs Used for Shopping   130
Verbs Used in a Bank   134
Using the Present Progressive Tense   136
Verbs Used for Outdoor Activities   138
Verbs Used for Activities in Public Places   141

Using the Present Perfect Tense 143
Verbs Used for Leisure Activities 146
Verbs Used for Cooking 148
Giving Directions 151

PART IV   Adverbs   153

Unit 14 **Adverbs of Place, Time, and Frequency** 155
Adverbs of Place 155
Adverbs of Time 159
Adverbs of Frequency 161

Unit 15 **Adverbs of Manner** 163
Forming Adverbs from Adjectives 163
Comparing Adverbs 167

Unit 16 **Adverbs That Modify** 171
Adverbs That Modify Verbs 171
Adverbs That Modify Adjectives and Other Adverbs 173

Answer Key 177

Introduction

It is not easy to know how to start learning new words in a language that is not your native one. Most second-language learners depend on a favorite dictionary to get a quick translation of an unknown word; however, dictionaries are full of words that you may never need to use, or even to understand. How do you know which words to learn first?

One of the purposes of this book is to acquaint you with the English words that are most frequently used in the United States today—the words that people use every day with their family, friends, coworkers, and other people in the community in general. Presented here is a basic vocabulary of more than fifteen hundred words that have been carefully chosen because of their frequent appearance and usefulness in daily life. Once you have learned these words and mastered the structures in which they are used, you will be well equipped to add new words to this list, and you'll gradually continue to increase your working vocabulary.

The words of a language can be divided into two groups: content words and function words. Content words in English are either nouns—words that name people, places, things, or abstracts; adjectives—words that describe nouns; verbs—words that describe the actions of nouns; or adverbs—words that describe how an action is performed. Function words are those that form a structure that enables us to put the content words together to make sense. English function words include, for example, words such as *a*, *the*, *of*, *for*, and *and*—words that would be difficult to draw a picture of or to define in a word or two. Both types of words are extremely important for communication in any language.

The second purpose of this book is to provide practice in using content words within the framework of the function words that go with them. By practicing these two types of words together you will be not only learning new vocabulary but also using it correctly, enabling you to form meaningful sentences with a variety of individual words.

There are four sections in the book: Part I: Nouns, Part II: Adjectives, Part III: Verbs, and Part IV: Adverbs. Each of these parts contains a number of units, and each unit consists of special vocabulary for a certain topic and extensive exercises to practice it.

How to Use This Book

The best way to learn new vocabulary is to use it, both in speech and in writing. The exercises in this book are designed to give you that practice by encouraging you to write down exactly what you would say in the context provided. The repetition of words and structures in various types of exercises will help you remember the words and make them yours to use in real situations.

Following are suggestions to help you get the most out of this book:

1. Get a good dictionary, either bilingual or English only, to use as suggested below.
2. Copy on a separate sheet of paper the lists of words presented in each unit.
3. You will already know some of the words. Write a check by each one if you are certain of its meaning.
4. Look up in your dictionary the words that you do not know or are not sure of, and write a word in your language or a definition in English next to it on your paper.
5. Do the written exercises for the entire unit.
6. In the exercises that ask you to write personal sentences, try to use words that are new to you. Of course, if the new words do not fit, use words that you already know.
7. Compare your answers with those in the Answer Key at the back of the book. For the exercises that require personal answers, you may wish to ask a native speaker friend to read your answers to see if they are correct.
8. Go back to your original list, cover up the translations or definitions that you first wrote, and see if you now know all the new words.
9. Try writing more sentences, using the same patterns used in the exercises, to further practice the words that you haven't completely mastered so far.
10. Keep practicing!

PART I

NOUNS

Nouns are the words we use to name all the things we know about, have, see, hear, taste, smell, or feel. This includes words for people, such as *man, teacher,* and *friend.* It includes words for places, such as *city, kitchen,* and *street.* It includes words for things, such as *ball, tree,* and *computer.* And it includes words for things we know exist but can't touch, such as *idea, air, pollution,* and *strength.*

Many nouns can be counted—one friend, two friends, for example. These nouns have plural forms, which in English usually means they have an *-s* added to the end, according to certain set spelling and pronunciation patterns. A few nouns have "irregular" plurals—instead of ending in *-s,* they have forms that have survived from earlier forms of English or were adapted from other languages. Examples of these include *women, men, children, media,* and *phenomena.*

Other nouns cannot be counted—*air, wind,* and *pollution,* for example. They have no plural forms, are used with singular verbs, and are called "noncount" nouns. But noncount nouns can also be things that we can count! First, there are those that it would take a lifetime to count, so we call them by a more general noncount noun, such as *hair, sugar,* or *flour.* And then there are those that we categorize in general groups that are named by noncount nouns, such as *furniture, mail, silverware,* and *china.* Of course we can count *chairs, tables,* or *beds,* but the general category *furniture* is never made plural. The noncount noun *mail* includes the *letters* and *cards* that we can count. English has a lot of these words.

One thing that singular, plural, and noncount nouns have in common is that they can all, in certain situations, be preceded by the article *the. The* before a noun indicates that both the speaker and the hearer know exactly *which one* of the nouns is being referred to. "*The* groceries are in *the* car," for example, informs the hearer that "the groceries that we just bought" are in "the car that we have."

When you know the patterns for using nouns, you can add new ones to your vocabulary every day and know you are using them correctly. Have fun with nouns!

Unit 1	# People and Places

Words for People

Members of the Family

Review the words in the following list:

aunt	husband
brother	mother
cousin	nephew
daughter	niece
father	sister
granddaughter	son
grandfather	uncle
grandmother	wife
grandson	

To identify a member of the family of someone's husband or wife, add *in-law* after the relationship word. For example, a man's *mother-in-law* is his wife's mother.

brother-in-law	mother-in-law
daughter-in-law	sister-in-law
father-in-law	son-in-law

 **exercise   1-1**

Fill in each blank with a word from one of the preceding lists.

1. My father's mother is my _____.

2. Her husband is my _____.

3. My mother's sister is my _____.

4. Her husband is my _____.

3

5. Their daughter is my _____.

6. My daughter's husband is my _____.

7. I am a _____, _____,

   _____, _____,

   _____, and _____.

8. I have a _____, _____,

   _____, _____,

   _____, and _____.

Categories for People

Review the words in the following list:

acquaintance	girl	neighbor
baby	guest	teenager
boy	host	visitor
child	hostess	woman
friend	man	

exercise   1-2

Match each word from the list on the left with its description on the right.

_____ 1. baby   a. a person who lives or works near where you live or work

_____ 2. boy   b. a grown-up female

_____ 3. child   c. a person between the ages of thirteen and nineteen

_____ 4. friend   d. someone you know well and like

_____ 5. girl   e. a grown-up male

_____ 6. man   f. a person under the age of two

_____ 7. neighbor   g. a young male

_____ 8. teenager   h. a young female

_____ 9. woman   i. a person under the age of thirteen

Names of Workers

Review the words in the following list:

accountant	driver	pharmacist
actor	employer	photographer
actress	engineer	pianist
adviser	firefighter	pilot
architect	football player	police officer
artist	guide	professor
beautician	hostess	programmer
boss	janitor	pupil
carpenter	journalist	reporter
cleaner	lawyer	sales assistant
cook	mail carrier	singer
customer	manager	stewardess
dancer	mechanic	student
dentist	military officer	teacher
designer	nurse	technician
director	painter	writer
doctor	patient	

exercise   1-3

Circle the word that best completes each sentence.

1. When I am sick I see a _____.

   lawyer   carpenter   doctor   police officer

2. The person who gives traffic tickets is a _____.

   singer   lawyer   firefighter   police officer

3. The person who lives near my house is my _____.

   firefighter   neighbor   military officer   journalist

4. Medicines are prepared at the drugstore by a _____.

   mechanic   nurse   pharmacist   sales assistant

5. If I have a toothache, I see a _____.

   janitor   doctor   dentist   technician

Parts of the Body

Review the words in the following list:

ankle	heel
arm	hip
cheeks	knee
chest	leg
chin	lips
ears	mouth
elbow	neck
eyes	nose
face	shoulders
fingers	stomach
foot	thumb
hair	toes
hand	waist
head	wrist

exercise	1-4

Fill in the blanks.

1. The _____, _____, _____, _____, _____,

   _____, _____, _____, and _____ are on the *head*.

2. The *elbow* is in the middle of the _____.

3. The _____ is in the middle of the *leg*.

4. The _____ is between the *hand* and the *arm*.

5. The _____ is between the *foot* and the *leg*.

6. The *foot* has five _____; the *hand* has four _____ and one _____.

7. The *shoulders* are between the _____ and the _____ .

8. The _____ is above the *stomach* and below the *chest*.

Words for Places

Outside Places

Review the words in the following list:

airport	gas station	railroad
apartment	grass	river
area	grocery store	road
bank	highway	school
barbershop	hill	shopping center
beach	hospital	shops
building	hotel	sidewalk
bus stop	house	street
church	land	suburb
city	library	sun
corner	moon	town
country	mountain	traffic light
drugstore	neighborhood	train station
farm	ocean	tree
florist	park	yard
garden	post office	

exercise   1-5

Circle the word that does not *belong in each group.*

1. airport   train station   road   bus stop

2. library   ocean   mountain   river

3. drugstore   grocery store   florist   sun

4. post office   bank   library   farm

5. street   highway   apartment   road

6. moon   house   hotel   apartment

7. tree   post office   yard   garden

8. church   highway   library   school

exercise **1-6**

What places do you go to every day?

_____   _____

_____   _____

_____   _____

_____   _____

exercise **1-7**

What places do you go to once or twice a week?

_____   _____

_____   _____

_____   _____

exercise **1-8**

What places do you go to occasionally (sometimes)?

_____   _____

_____   _____

_____   _____

exercise **1-9**

Where do you never go?

_____   _____

_____   _____

Inside Places

Review the words in the following list:

attic	front door
back door	hall
basement	kitchen
bathroom	laundry room
bedroom	library
ceiling	living room
classroom	office
corner	restaurant
department store	second floor
dining room	store
first floor	wall
floor	window

exercise   1-10

Write the name of the place or places where each of the following things is usually found.

1. bathtub _____

2. bed _____

3. bedspread _____

4. blackboard _____

5. blanket _____

6. book _____

7. bookshelf _____

8. buffet _____

9. bulletin board _____

10. chair _____

11. closet _____

12. coffeemaker _____

13. coffee table _____

14. computer _____

15. copier _____

16. counter   _____

17. cup   _____

18. desk   _____

19. detergent   _____

20. dish   _____

21. dishwasher   _____

22. dresser   _____

23. dryer   _____

24. elevator   _____

25. escalator   _____

26. facecloth   _____

27. fax machine   _____

28. filing cabinet   _____

29. fireplace   _____

30. fork   _____

31. garbage disposer   _____

32. glass   _____

33. knife   _____

34. lamp   _____

35. magazine   _____

36. microwave oven   _____

37. napkin   _____

38. newspaper   _____

39. night table   _____

40. notebook   _____

41. pan   _____

42. paper _____

43. pen _____

44. pencil _____

45. pillow _____

46. pillowcasc _____

47. plate _____

48. printer _____

49. refrigerator _____

50. saucer _____

51. shcct _____

52. shower _____

53. sink _____

54. soap _____

55. sofa _____

56. spoon _____

57. stairway _____

58. stove _____

59. table _____

60. tea towel _____

61. telephone _____

62. toaster _____

63. toilet _____

64. towel _____

65. TV set _____

66. washing machine _____

Unit 2

Singular, Plural, and Noncount Nouns

Using Singular Nouns

English nouns can be divided into two categories: *count nouns* and *noncount nouns.*

A count noun is *singular* when there is *one* of the person, place, or thing it names.

When a noun is singular, use *a* or *an* before it. Use *a* if it begins with a *consonant* sound; use *an* if it begins with a *vowel* sound.

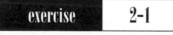

exercise | **2-1**

Write a *or* an *before each of the following singular nouns.*

1. _____ brother

2. _____ aunt

3. _____ artist

4. _____ employer

5. _____ janitor

6. _____ professor

7. _____ patient

8. _____ engineer

9. _____ reporter

10. _____ stewardess

11. _____ sister

12. _____ uncle

13. _____ dentist

14. _____ driver

15. _____ actor

16. _____ adviser

17. _____ accountant

18. _____ technician

19. _____ architect

20. _____ actress

21. _____ cheek

22. _____ chest

23. _____ leg

24. _____ ear

25. _____ mouth

26. _____ area

27. _____ apartment

28. _____ river

29. _____ bus stop

30. _____ basement

31. _____ elbow

32. _____ arm

33. _____ ankle

34. _____ nose

35. _____ eye

36. _____ library

37. _____ house

38. _____ ocean

39. _____ airport

40. _____ attic

Use *a* or *an* before a singular noun to answer the question *"What . . . ?"*

What do you do?	I'm **a** secretary.	I'm **an** actor.
What is it?	It's **a** banana.	It's **an** apple.
What do you want?	I want **a** house.	I want **an** apartment.

Use the number *one* before a singular noun to answer the question *"How many . . . ?"*

| How many cars do you have? | We have **one** car. |
| How many English classes are there? | There is **one** class. |

Use *"There is . . ."* before a singular noun to indicate that it exists.

There is an accountant in my family.
There is a library on the corner.
There is only one bus stop on this street.

exercise   2-2

Look at page 13 of this book and answer the following questions. Be careful in your choice of a, an, *or* one *before each singular noun.*

1. What do you have in your hands?

   _____

2. What is there at the very end of this book?

   _____

3. In the word *Contents,* what is there between the first *n* and the *e*?

   _____

4. How many *e*'s are there in the word *Contents*?

   _____

Words for Groups of People

Some singular nouns name groups of people who have the same interest. These are called *collective* nouns. Use a collective noun with a singular verb form. Observe the following examples:

band	company
choir	family
chorus	government
class	orchestra
committee	team

exercise   2-3

Fill in each blank with a word from the previous list. Be sure to include a *or* an *in each blank before the noun.*

1. A group of people who take a course together is _____.

2. A group of people who play musical instruments together can be

   _____ or _____ .

3. A group of people who form a business is _____.

4. People who are related by blood are _____.

5. A group of people who play together to win a game or sport is _____.

6. A group of people who control public policy in a country is _____.

7. A group of people who make plans for a larger group is called _____.

8. A group of people who sing together is _____ or

_____.

Using Plural Nouns

A count noun is *plural* when there is *more than one* of the person, place, or thing it names. To make a singular noun plural:

- Add -*s*:

one tree	three tree**s**
one word	four word**s**
one sister	two sister**s**

- Add -*es* to a few words that end in -*o*:

one echo	two echo**es**
one mosquito	three mosquito**es**
one tomato	four tomato**es**
one hero	four hero**es**
one potato	two potato**es**
one tornado	two tornado**es**

- Add -*es* to nouns that end in -*ch*, -*sh*, -*ss*, and -*x*:

one beach	two beach**es**
one dish	four dish**es**
one dress	two dress**es**
one fax	three fax**es**

- Add -*ies* to nouns that end in a consonant followed by -*y*, after dropping the -*y*:

one city	two cit**ies**
one country	four countr**ies**
one family	two famil**ies**
one puppy	six pupp**ies**

- Add -*ves* to nouns that end in -*f* or -*fe*, after dropping the -*f* or -*fe*:

one calf	two cal**ves**
one half	two hal**ves**
one leaf	three lea**ves**
one knife	five kni**ves**

- Use an irregular form for certain nouns:

one child	two child**ren**
one man	four m**en**
one person	three pe**ople**
one tooth	four t**ee**th
one mouse	three m**ice**
one woman	three wom**en**
one foot	two f**ee**t

- Use the singular form for the plural for certain nouns:

one deer	three deer
one sheep	four sheep
one fish	two fish

exercise   2-4

Write the plural form of each of the following nouns.

1. brother   _____

2. daughter   _____

3. wife   _____

4. baby   _____

5. child   _____

6. man   _____

7. woman   _____

8. teenager   _____

9. artist   _____

10. customer   _____

11. student   _____

12. actress   _____

13. boss   _____

14. nurse   _____

15. eye   _____

16. ear   _____

17. toe   _____

18. church   _____

19. city   _____

20. library   _____

21. bus stop   _____

22. post office   _____

23. window   _____

24. glass   _____

25. knife _____

26. fork _____

27. stove _____

28. facecloth _____

exercise	2-5

Write the plural form of each of the following collective *nouns.*

1. band _____

2. choir _____

3. chorus _____

4. class _____

5. committee _____

6. family _____

7. government _____

8. orchestra _____

9. team _____

Use *are there* and a plural noun in a question to ask if any exist and how many:

> **Are there any** cars in your driveway?
> How many cars **are there**?
> How many houses **are there** on this street?
> How many pages **are there** in this book?

Use *there are* followed by any number from *two* on up before a plural noun to tell how many of them exist:

> **There are two** cars in the driveway.
> **There are ten** houses on this street.
> **There are 208** pages in this book.

Use *there are* before the word *no* when it indicates *zero*. *No* is followed by a plural noun:

> **There are no** cars in the driveway.
> **There are no** houses on this street.

Not any can be used instead of *no* to indicate *zero*:

There are **not any** cars in the driveway.   There are**n't any** cars in the driveway.
There are **not any** houses on this street.   There are**n't any** houses on this street.

Words for Clothes and Accessories

Review the following examples:

For Men and Women	Usually for Women	Usually for Men
belt	blouse	necktie/bow tie
cap	bracelet	tuxedo
chain	dress	
coat	handbag/purse/pocketbook	
earring	necklace	
hat	nightgown	
jacket	skirt	
raincoat		
ring		
robe		
scarf		
shirt		
suit		
sweater		
sweatshirt		
T-shirt		
umbrella		
wallet		
watch		

exercise   2-6

*Select twelve items from the preceding list, and write how many of each item there are in your closets and drawers.
Use* There are *to begin each sentence.*

1. _____

2. _____

3. _____

4. _____

5. _____

6. _____

7. _____

8. _____

9. _____

10. _____

11. _____

12. _____

Pairs

Some clothing items are usually in two parts, which are sometimes separate, such as two *gloves*, and sometimes connected, such as *pants*. The nouns are plural. One set of two parts is a *pair*. A *pair of shoes*, for example, is two shoes, one for the left foot and one for the right. A *pair of pants* is one item, with two legs.

Review the following examples of *pairs*:

For Men and Women	Usually for Women
earrings	
glasses	
sunglasses	
gloves	
pajamas	
pants	
jeans	
shorts	
sweatpants	
shoes	
boots	flats
sandals	high heels
slippers	
socks	stockings
	tights

exercise   **2-7**

How many pairs *do you have in your closets and drawers?*

I have one pair of _____, one pair of _____, and one

pair of _____.

I have _____ pairs of _____,

_____ pairs of _____, and

_____ pairs of _____.

Quantities

To tell an approximate number of plural items there are, use:

some	=	more than one
a few	=	three or four
a lot of/ lots of/ many	=	a large number of/plenty of/enough
not many	=	a small number of
too many	=	more than is good or necessary

I have **some** tickets for the ball game.
There are **a few** seats in the front row.
A lot of people are going to the game.
There are **not many** seats.
There are **too many** people here.

exercise	2-8

Look at all of the lists of nouns for people, places, and things to answer the following questions.

1. What do you have *some* of? Begin each answer with *I have . . .*

   _____

   _____

   _____

   _____

   _____

2. What are there *a lot of* outside? Begin each answer with *There are . . .*

   _____

   _____

   _____

   _____

   _____

3. What are there *not many* of in the place where you live? Begin each answer with *There are . . .*

   _____

   _____

   _____

   _____

_____

_____

4. What do you see *a few* of right now? Begin each answer with *I see . . .*

_____

_____

_____

_____

_____

5. What do you have *too many* of? Begin each answer with *I have . . .*

_____

_____

_____

_____

_____

Words for Food

Review the following words that name things to eat or drink. These nouns can be either singular or plural.

apple	nut
avocado	orange
banana	pea
bean	pear
carrot	potato
cherry	potato chip
doughnut	salad
drink	sandwich
egg	snack
grape	soda
hamburger	steak
hot dog	tomato
meal	vegetable

exercise   2-9

Write one of the following words or groups of words in each blank, depending on whether the nouns are singular or plural.

a   an   one   some   a lot of   a few   no   any   two

1. He eats _____ egg and _____ doughnut for breakfast.

2. I like to have _____ apple or _____ orange in the afternoon.

3. Would you like _____ peas and _____ carrots?

4. She wants _____ sandwich and _____ potato chips.

5. I want _____ banana.

6. We would like _____ hot dogs, please.

7. There aren't _____ hamburgers.

8. She is going to the store to buy _____ tomatoes.

9. She's going to buy _____ steaks for dinner.

10. I didn't order _____ salad; I ordered _____ vegetables instead.

Using Noncount Nouns

Many words for food are *noncount* nouns. Some examples are the words in the following list:

Liquids	Dry Items	Meat	Dairy Products	Vegetables	Other
beer	bread	bacon	butter	broccoli	cake
coffee	cereal	beef	cheese	cauliflower	candy
cream	flour	chicken	ice cream	corn	fruit
gravy	rice	fish	yogurt	eggplant	jam
juice	sugar	meat		lettuce	jelly
milk	toast	pork		spinach	pepper
sauce				squash	pie
soup					popcorn
tea					salt
water					
wine					

Many personal care items are also named by noncount nouns. Review the words in the following list:

aftershave lotion	lotion
bath gel	perfume
conditioner	shampoo
cream	shaving cream
fingernail polish	soap
fingernail polish remover	toothpaste

Use *is there any* before a noncount noun to ask if it exists:

> **Is there any** rice in the cupboard?
> **Is there any** fruit in the refrigerator?
> **Is there any** soap in the bathroom?

Use *how much* followed by a noncount noun plus *is there* to ask the amount of it that exists:

> **How much** ice cream **is there**?
> **How much** cereal **is there**?
> **How much** water **is there**?
> **How much** shampoo **is there**?

To tell the approximate amount of a noncount noun, use:

some	=	more than nothing
a lot of	=	a large amount of
a little	=	a small amount of
not much	=	a very small amount of
no/not any	=	nothing

> There is **some** ice cream in the freezer.
> There is **a lot of** fruit in the bowl.
> There is **a little** cereal in the box.
> There is **not much** shampoo.
> There is **no** water./There is**n't any** water.

---

exercise   **2-10**

Use words from the noncount noun food list to answer the following questions.

1. What is there a lot of in your refrigerator?

   _____

2. Is there any candy in the cupboard?

   _____

3. How much bread is there in the kitchen?

   _____

4. Is there any popcorn in the cupboard?

   _____

5. Is there too much of anything?

   _____

exercise   2-11

Use words from the noncount noun personal care items list to answer the following questions.

1. Is there any shampoo in your bathroom?

   _____

2. How much toothpaste is there?

   _____

3. What else is there?

   _____

To tell the exact amount of a noncount noun, use the singular or plural of the container of the item, the weight of the item, or the number of *pieces* or *servings* of it there are:

a can of soup	three cans of soup
a cup of coffee	two cups of coffee
a glass of milk	four glasses of milk
a bowl of cereal	a few bowls of cereal
one spoonful of sugar	two spoonfuls of sugar
one serving of spinach	three servings of spinach
a piece of meat	two pieces of meat
a tube of toothpaste	two tubes of toothpaste

Types of Containers	Weights and Measures	Serving Sizes
bag	cup	bite
bar	drop	piece
bottle	gallon	sip
bowl	ounce	slice
box	pint	
case	pound	
cup	quart	
glass	spoonful	
jar	tablespoon	
package	teaspoon	
plate		
tube		

exercise   2-12

Look at your answers to Exercise 2-10. Change the approximate amounts of each item to exact amounts and write the complete sentences here.

1. _____

2. _____

3. _____

4. _____

5. _____

exercise   2-13

Look at your answers to Exercise 2-11. Change the approximate amounts of each item to exact amounts and write the complete sentences here.

1. _____

2. _____

3. _____

exercise   2-14

Circle all of the words or sets of words that could be used in each blank.

1. There is _____ bread on the table.

   a little   a   a lot of   some   three slices of   no   a slice of

2. There are _____ bread on the table.

   a little   a few   some   three slices of   an   no

3. We need _____ ice cream.

   a little   some   three bowls of   many   a gallon of   two quarts of

4. She drank _____ milk.

   a glass of   three glasses of   a few   some   a little

5. They're going to buy _____ rice.

   some   a little   a few   two bags of   a   an   one

6. I would like to have _____ lettuce on my sandwich.

   a piece of   two pieces of   a little   a   two   some

7. He ate _____ cake.

   some   a piece of   piece of   two pieces of   three   a lot of

8. There is _____ pie in the refrigerator.

    some   **a piece of**   **piece of**   **two pieces of**   **no**   **three**

9. There are _____ cups of coffee here.

    a   **two**   **one**   **a few**   **a little**   **some**   **no**   **any**

10. I drink _____ juice every morning.

    a   **two**   **a glass of**   **two glasses of**   **some**   **a lot of**   **too many**

Words for Groups of Individual Items

Other *noncount* nouns include words that represent groups of individual items. The individual items can be counted, but the word that represents the entire group cannot.

Furniture	Mail	Jewelry	Money	Information	Trash
bed	advertisement	bracelet	dime	brochure	boxes
chair	bill	earrings	dollar bill	notice	packaging
desk	letter	necklace	five	pamphlet	used items
dresser	postcard	pin	nickel	report	
nightstand	penny				
sofa	quarter				
table	ten				
	twenty				

For a Desk	For Cooking	Hardware	Medicine	Makeup	Entertainment
paper	pan	hammer	capsule	blush	game
pen	pot	nail	drop	eyebrow pencil	movie
pencil	spatula	pliers	pill	foundation	party
scissors	spoon	screw	tablet	lipstick	radio
tape		screwdriver		mascara	show
		wrench		powder	television

There is *some* furniture.   There are three chairs.
You have *a little* mail.   You have two letters and a postcard.
She has *a lot of* jewelry.   She has five necklaces, four bracelets, and
                                       twenty pairs of earrings.

He has *a little* money.   He has a ten, a five, and three quarters.
We got *some* information.   We got a brochure and two reports.
There is *too much* trash.   There are boxes, old clothes, broken toys,
                                       worn-out tires, and broken dishes.

exercise   **2-15**

Answer each question.

1. How much furniture do you have?

   _____

2. What mail do you usually receive?

   _____

3. What jewelry do you like to wear?

   _____

4. How much money do you have in your pocket?

   _____

5. What do you throw in the trash every day?

   _____

There are many things that cannot be counted. Like all noncount nouns, words for these things do not have plural forms. Review the words in the following list:

advice	help	poverty
air	homework	rain
beauty	housework	sickness
cold	intelligence	snow
courage	kindness	strength
darkness	light	water
health	news	wealth
heat	pollution	work

There is some housework to do.
There is a lot of news.
There is a little snow in the mountains.
There is not much heat in the house.
There is too much rain.

Do *not* use *a, an, one, many,* or any number with a noncount noun.

exercise   **2-16**

Circle all of the words that can be used in each blank space.

1. We have _____ help.

   many   **a little**   **four**   **an**

2. There is _____ heat.

   no   **too many**   **some**   **a little**

3. They need _____ advice.

    some   **an**   **not many**   **a lot of**

4. She has _____ work.

    many   **some**   **a little**   **a**   **an**

5. There is _____ poverty in the city.

    a   **too much**   **not many**   **a lot of**

exercise   2-17

Answer the following questions. Use no, not much, some, a little, a lot of, *or* too much *before each noncount noun.*

1. Do you have news about your friends in your country? Begin your answer with *I have . . .*

   _____

2. Is there work available in this city? Begin your answer with *There is . . .*

   _____

3. How much rain is there here in the summer? Begin your answer with *There is . . .*

   _____

4. Do you need advice? Begin your answer with *I need . . .*

   _____

5. Is there pollution in your area? Begin your answer with *There is . . .*

   _____

Using Articles with Singular, Plural, and Noncount Nouns

The indefinite articles *a* and *an* are used before singular nouns that refer to any one of that person, place, or thing:

> **A** clock is **an** instrument that marks time.
> **A** watch is **a** clock that you wear on your wrist.

The previous sentences do not name a specific clock or watch; they refer to clocks and watches in general.

The articles *a* and *an* can refer to a specific singular noun to tell or ask someone about it for the first time:

I have **a** clock that is 150 years old.
Her boyfriend gave her **a** watch for her birthday.

There are no indefinite articles for plural and noncount nouns. To refer to people, places, or things in general, *no* word (Ø) is placed before the plural or noncount noun:

Ø Clocks are instruments that mark time.
Ø Mail includes anything that can be delivered by the post officc.

No word (Ø) can refer to a plural or noncount noun to tell or ask someone about it for the first time:

Her boyfriend brings her Ø flowers every week.
You got Ø mail this morning.

exercise   **2-18**

Fill in each blank with one of the following.

     a   **an**   **Ø**

1. I am going to buy _____ orange.

2. They sell _____ oranges at the market on the corner.

3. Do you have _____ fruit?

4. Yes, we have _____ oranges and _____ apples.

5. Where do they sell _____ furniture in this city?

6. I'm looking for _____ table, _____ chairs, and _____ desk.

7. We need _____ information.

8. Can you give me _____ advice?

9. Do you have _____ kitchen equipment?

10. I want to buy _____ pot and _____ frying pan.

The definite article *the* is used before a singular noun, a plural noun, or a noncount noun to refer to a specific person, place, or thing.

The is used when the speaker and the listener both know which particular item is being referred to:

She showed me **the** watch *her boyfriend gave her* for her birthday.
The flowers *he sent her* were beautiful.
The furniture *I bought* was cheap.

exercise   2-19

Fill in each blank with one of the following:

a   an   Ø   the

1. I bought _____ radio yesterday.

2. Where is _____ radio (you bought)?

3. We have _____ kitchen equipment on sale.

4. Where is _____ kitchen equipment (that you have on sale)?

5. I love _____ flowers.

6. Are these _____ flowers your friend sent you?

7. Where is _____ medicine the doctor gave you?

8. Are these _____ pills you are taking?

9. He is looking for _____ information.

10. He didn't like _____ information he got from the company.

exercise   2-20

Write two sentences that tell about one thing you have. Use a *or* an *in the first sentence to introduce it. Use* the *in the second sentence to tell more about it.*

1. _____

2. _____

_____

exercise   2-21

Write two sentences that tell about something you have more than one of. Use Ø *in the first sentence to introduce the items. Use* the *in the second sentence to tell more about them.*

1. _____

2. _____

_____

exercise   2-22

Write two sentences that tell about a noncount item you have. Use Ø in the first sentence to introduce it. Use the in the second sentence to tell more about it.

1. _____

2. _____

   _____

The is used when there is only one possible reference:

> I left my keys in **the** car. (the car I drive)
> Please put the bags in **the** kitchen. (the only kitchen in the house)
> Please feed **the** dog. (the dog we own)

exercise   2-23

Fill in each blank with one of the following:

   a   an   the   Ø

1. We bought _____ car last night.

2. _____ cars are expensive.

3. _____ car we bought is a convertible.

4. Do you like _____ convertibles?

5. Do you like _____ convertible we bought?

Using Demonstrative Pronouns with Singular, Plural, and Noncount Nouns

There are four *demonstrative pronouns*: *this, that, these,* and *those. This* and *these* refer to nouns that are close enough to touch, things that are *here.*

Use *this* before a singular or noncount noun; use *these* before a plural noun:

> **This** watch is the one I like.
> **These** watches are very expensive.
> **This** jewelry is very expensive.

That and *those* refer to nouns that are not close enough to touch, things that are *there*:

> Do you like **that** dress in the store window?
> **Those** dresses in front are very pretty.
> **That** information about the prices is not correct.

exercise   2-24

Fill in each blank with this, that, these, *or* those.

1. _____ book in my hands is very interesting.

2. What are _____ things he is carrying?

3. We're going to see _____ new movie at the Odeon.

4. Come here and look at _____ pictures with me.

5. Who is _____ girl over there?

6. Who are _____ girls over there?

7. Hi, I'm Sally and _____ are my friends, Amy and Courtney.

8. I'm wearing _____ sweater because I'm cold.

Proper Nouns

A *proper noun* is the name that has been given to a person, a group of people, a place, or a thing. The names of religions and of languages are proper nouns. A proper noun is written with a capital letter at the beginning of each word. Here are some examples of proper nouns:

Betty	Garden Club
John Clark	Planning Committee
Capitol Hill	February
Oak Street	French
Monday	Ireland
The Daily Mirror	

Longer names and titles of books often have prepositions and articles, which are not written with capital letters, except when those words appear at the beginning:

The University of the East   *A Boy's Life in the Country*

exercise 3-1

Change lowercase letters to capital letters where necessary.

1. She's reading a book called *a guide to good manners.*

2. We have to go to the springfield library on monday.

3. They are from italy, and they don't speak spanish.

4. david is going to go to wilson academy for boys in september.

exercise   **3-2**

Write the proper names of people, places, or things you know.

1. A person I know: _____

2. The street I live on: _____

3. The name of a school: _____

4. The language I speak: _____

5. The country I'm from: _____

6. A river in my country: _____

7. A newspaper: _____

8. A book I like: _____

9. Today's day: _____

10. The date of my birthday: _____

11. A group I belong to: _____

12. A restaurant I like: _____

Possessive Nouns and Pronouns

Possessive Nouns

A *possessive noun* indicates that the person, place, or thing named is the owner or holder of the noun that follows. It answers the question *Whose . . . ?* A possessive noun can be used before a singular noun, a plural noun, or a noncount noun.

It can be a proper noun followed by -'s:

Emily's dress **Bill's** shoes. **Susan's** ice cream

A possessive noun can be a common noun followed by -'s:

the **teacher's** desk the **man's** glasses a **friend's** mail

When two or more people own or have something, the plural noun is followed by an apostrophe if it ends in -s:

the **teachers'** party the **students'** books my **friends'** health

If the plural form does not end in -s, it is followed by -'s:

the **men's** cars the **children's** class the **people's** money

exercise	4-1

Write a phrase with a possessive noun for each item listed.

1. car/my sister _____

2. hats/the men _____

3. party/the children _____

4. office/the doctor _____

5. apartment/the girls _____

6. class/Miss Smith _____

7. school/Ben Lindsay _____

8. meeting/the ladies _____

Look at some photographs of your family and friends. Write five things you see, and indicate to whom they belong.

     EXAMPLES: That's Debbie's dog.
                  Those are my sister's shoes.

1. _____

2. _____

3. _____

4. _____

5. _____

Possessive Pronouns

A *possessive pronoun* can be used in place of a possessive noun. A possessive pronoun can be used before a singular, plural, or noncount noun. These are the possessive pronouns:

my	it belongs to **me**
your	it belongs to **you**
his	it belongs to **him**
her	it belongs to **her**
its	it belongs to **an animal, a group, or an organization**
our	it belongs to **me and one or more other people**
your	it belongs to **you and one or more other people**
their	it belongs to **one or more other people, animals, groups, or organizations**

I drive **my** car to work.
Do you have **your** driver's license?
Bob gave me **his** telephone number.   He gave me **his** telephone number.
Jane doesn't have **her** ticket.   She doesn't have **her** ticket.
Susan and I bought **our** supplies.   We bought **our** supplies.
Do you and Sam have **your** books?   Do you have **your** books?

exercise   4-3

Look at your answers to Exercise 4-1. Change the possessive nouns to possessive pronouns.

1. _____

2. _____

3. _____

4. _____

5. _____

6. _____

7. _____

8. _____

exercise   4-4

Look at your answers to Exercise 4-2. Change the possessive nouns to possessive pronouns.

1. _____

2. _____

3. _____

4. _____

5. _____

Review of Singular, Plural, and Noncount Nouns

These are similarities between *singular, plural,* and *noncount* nouns:

- All can follow *the*:

the letter	**the** letters	**the** mail

- All can follow a *possessive noun*:

John's letter	**John's** letters	**John's** mail

- All can follow a *possessive pronoun*:

his letter	**his** letters	**his** mail

These are similarities between *singular* and *noncount* nouns:

- Both can follow *this*:

this letter	**this** mail

- Both are followed by *a singular verb*:

The letter **is** here.   The mail **is** here.

These are similarities between *plural* and *noncount* nouns:

- They can follow *no*:

no letters	**no** mail

- They can follow *not any*:

not any letters	**not any** mail

- They can follow *some*:

some letters	**some** mail

- They can follow *a lot of* or *lots of*:

  a lot of letters   **a lot of** mail
  lots of letters   **lots of** mail

- They can be used with no word (Ø) before them, to make a general statement:

  Ø Letters are stamped at the post office.
  Ø Mail is stamped at the post office.

These are characteristics of *singular* nouns only:

- They can follow *a* or *an*:

  a banana   **an** orange

These are characteristics of *plural* nouns only:

- They can follow *a few*:

  a few bananas   **a few** letters

- They can follow *not many* or *too many*:

  not many bananas   **too many** letters

These are characteristics of *noncount* nouns only:

- They can follow *a little*:

  a little fruit   **a little** mail

- They can follow *not much* or *too much*:

  not much fruit   **too much** mail

exercise   5-1

Circle the word that correctly fills in each blank.

1. There are _____ people in this room.

   a   **one**   **too many**   **too much**

2. There is _____ artist in our family.

   a   **some**   **a lot of**   **an**   **these**

3. Do you have _____ books I gave you?

   a   **too many**   **the**   **too much**   **an**

4. _____ airplanes are making a lot of noise.

   Too much   **Ø**   **Those**   **This**   **A little**

5. I'm hoping you can give me _____ advice.

   too many　　　**an**　　　　**one**　　　　**three**　　　　**a little**

6. Our neighbors have _____ children.

   too much　　　**a lot of**　　　**a little**　　　**one**　　　　**a**

7. The doctor says that I eat _____ salt.

   too many　　　**a few**　　　　**a**　　　　**too much**　　　**this**

8. There are _____ tickets available.

   too much　　　**this**　　　　**that**　　　　**no**　　　　　**a little**

9. _____ apartment is near my house.

   John's　　　　**A few**　　　　**A lot of**　　　**Some**　　　　**A**

10. We would like _____ help.

    some　　　　**a few**　　　　**a**　　　　**many**　　　　**one**

---

exercise　　5-2

Match the words in the left column with the nouns in the right column.

1. one   bottles
   four   bottle

2. these   information
   that   letters

3. a few   pills
   a little   medicine

4. too much   sugar
   one   spoonfuls
   a few   spoonful

5. too many   furniture
   not much   chairs
   a   chair

6. a   jewelry
   these   necklace
   a little   earrings

7. that   vegetables
   those   fruit

8. There is a   hardware
   There are   nail
   There is   screws

9. There is one   water
   There are no   lights
   There is no   lamp

10. Here is your   letters
    There are no   letter

Verbs Used as Nouns

The *present participle* form of a verb can be used as a noun to be the subject of a sentence, or the object of a verb or a preposition. Present participles are called *gerunds* when they are used as nouns. (See page 96 for the formation of *present participles.*)

Gerund as Subject	**Gerund as Object**
Walking is good exercise.	We enjoy **walking**.
Eating well is important.	I like **eating** at this restaurant.
Working here is interesting.	She is tired of **working** here.
Playing with other children makes her happy.	He talks about **playing** with other children.

exercise 6-1

Fill in each blank with the gerund *form of the verb indicated.*

1. We are very tired of (wait) _____ for her.

2. (drive) _____ at night can be dangerous.

3. Do you like (live) _____ here?

4. They argued about her (cook) _____.

5. (study) _____ at the university gave him a good background.

6. We're not afraid of (stay) _____ alone.

exercise	6-2

Write sentences that change the verbs to nouns.

1. sing _____

2. drink _____

3. sleep _____

4. write _____

5. study _____

More Specific Nouns

There are many nouns that can replace general nouns to describe specific people, places, things, and ideas. Some examples follow. *Formal* indicates that the word is used mainly in writing. *Informal* indicates that the word is used mainly in conversation. *Slang* indicates that the word is very informal and that it is currently in style.

Words for People

boy: *a male child from birth to age eighteen*
My sister has three children, two **boys** and a girl.

bum: *a person who makes no effort to succeed*
She says her neighbor is a lazy **bum**.

dude: *a man who pays a lot of attention to his clothes*
Her new boyfriend is a handsome **dude**.

> *form of address to a friend (slang)*
> "**Dude**, we're having a party; come on over."

> *a stranger (slang)*
> I was walking down the street and that **dude** started talking to me.

gentleman: *a man with good manners*
Your brother is a perfect **gentleman**.

girl: *a female child from birth to age eighteen*
Your daughter is a lovely **girl**.

> *a young, unmarried woman*
> Our neighbor is a **girl** who is in law school.

guy: *a boy or man (informal)*
That **guy** who works at the drugstore is very helpful.

kid: *a male or female child (informal)*
There are a lot of **kids** in that family.

lady: *a woman with good manners*
The **lady** who lives across the street is a teacher.

man: *an adult male*
There are six **men** in the study group.

tomboy: *a girl who likes to play boys' games*
When I was ten years old I was a real **tomboy**.

woman: *an adult female*
I met an interesting **woman** at the meeting.

young lady: *a young woman with good manners*
The girls have grown up and are now charming **young ladies**.

youth: *a young man*
One of the **youths** at the convention gave a good speech.

young people
The **youth** of today have many opportunities.

exercise 7-1

Replace each italicized word with a more descriptive one from the previous list.

1. How many *children* does she have? _____

2. Did you notice the *boy* in the yellow shirt? _____

3. My brother's new girlfriend is an accomplished *girl*. _____

4. I don't want to be a *lazy person* who has no ambition. _____

Friends

acquaintance: *a person you have met but don't know very well*
An **acquaintance** of mine works in your office.

boyfriend: *a male who is someone's romantic interest*
Are you bringing your **boyfriend** to the party?

classmate: *a person who is in the same class with someone at school*
The school is so big, I don't even know all of my **classmates**.

colleague: *a person someone works with professionally*
All of my **colleagues** agree with the new plan.

companion: *a friend someone spends a lot of time with or lives with*
They are good **companions**; they go everywhere together.

coworker: *a person who works in the same place as someone*
She cannot get along with any of her **coworkers**.

fiancé: *a male to whom someone is engaged to be married*
He gave her a diamond ring, so now he's her **fiancé**.

fiancée: *a female to whom someone is engaged to be married*
She has been his **fiancée** for five years.

friend: *a person you know and like*
She has a lot of **friends** here.

girfriend: *a female who is someone's romantic interest*
I can't bring my **girlfriend**, because she lives in another city.

partner: *a companion*
Her **partner** works at the local nursery.

a person who co-owns a business with someone
My doctor is out of town, but his **partner** will see me.

roommate: *a person someone shares a room with*
We have a big room at college, so I have two **roommates**.

exercise   7-2

Fill in each blank with the most appropriate word from the previous list.

1. My aunt got engaged last month, and she is coming to visit with her new _____.

2. Her daughter, who is in college, complains that her _____ doesn't help clean the bathroom.

3. I don't like the boss's new program, but my _____ think it will work.

4. He's not a good friend of mine, just an _____.

Doctors

dentist: *a doctor who takes care of the teeth*
It's a good idea to see a **dentist** at least once a year.

dermatologist: *a skin specialist*
A **dermatologist** can help you with your allergies.

doctor/M.D.: *a person who has the degree of Doctor of Medicine, works to help sick people, and is licensed to prescribe medicine*
When you are sick, you should go to the **doctor**.

ear, nose, and throat doctor/E.N.T.: *a specialist for the ear, the nose, and the throat*
She sees an **E.N.T.** for her sinusitis.

eye doctor/ophthalmologist: *a specialist for eyes*
The **ophthalmologist** prescribed glasses for our son.

gastroenterologist: *a stomach specialist*
He is seeing a **gastroenterologist** to help cure his digestive problems.

general practitioner/G.P.: *an M.D. who treats most common diseases and ailments*
Our **G.P.** takes care of the whole family in one visit.

gynecologist: *a specialist in women's health*
Many women are checked by a **gynecologist** once a year.

obstetrician: *a specialist in the delivery of babies*
As soon as she suspected she was pregnant, she went to see an **obstetrician**.

orthodontist: *a dentist who specializes in straightening teeth*
The **orthodontist** fixed her crooked teeth, and now she has a beautiful smile.

orthopedist: *a specialist in bones*
When he broke his leg, the **orthopedist** put it in a cast.

pediatrician: *a specialist in children's health*
As soon as the baby was born he was examined by a **pediatrician**.

periodontist: *a dentist who specializes in gums*
The **periodontist** was able to help prevent gum recession in most patients.

podiatrist: *a specialist in feet*
The **podiatrist** told her not to wear high-heeled shoes.

specialist: *an M.D. who is an expert in one type of disease or part of the body*
Our G.P. recommended that we take our child to a **specialist**.

surgeon: *a specialist who performs major operations*
The **surgeon** was in the operating room for four hours.

 **exercise 7-3**

Match the health problem in the left column to the doctor in the right column. (Note: there are more problems than types of doctor.)

_____ 1. a woman thinks she is pregnant	a. dentist
_____ 2. a baby cries for three days	b. dermatologist
_____ 3. a child has red spots on his legs	c. pediatrician
_____ 4. a girl breaks her arm	d. eye doctor
_____ 5. a man needs glasses	e. obstetrician
_____ 6. a boy has earaches	f. E.N.T. doctor
_____ 7. a woman has a bad cold	g. G.P.
_____ 8. a girl's skin itches	h. orthopedist
_____ 9. a woman has a toothache	i. orthodontist
_____ 10. a girl needs braces for her teeth	

Artists

actor: *a male artist who performs in the theater, on television, or in the movies*
Which **actor** plays the main character in that film?

actress: *a female artist who performs in the theater, on television, or in the movies*
She is an **actress** who is able to play many different roles.

artist: *a person who works in a creative way*
The **artist** captured the beauty of the landscape.

designer: *an artist who works in clothing or home fashion*
She wears dresses only by her favorite **designer**.

musician: *an artist who composes or performs music*
He is an accomplished **musician** who writes all the songs he sings.

painter: *an artist who makes pictures with oil, watercolor, or another color medium*
The president's portrait was done by a famous **painter**.

photographer: *an artist who works with a camera to depict images*
We need a good **photographer** to capture the emotion of the celebration.

poet: *an artist who writes lyrical verses*
The **poet**'s words made me feel both happy and sad.

sculptor: *an artist who carves or models figures*
This **sculptor** prefers to work with marble.

writer: *an artist who puts words on paper to describe or narrate*
My favorite **writer** makes me feel that I am in the place he is describing.

exercise   7-4

Write the names of five artists you like, indicating the specific work of each one.

1. _____

2. _____

3. _____

4. _____

5. _____

Musicians

Review the words for musicians who play individual instruments:

cello	cellist
clarinet	clarinetist
drums	drummer
guitar	guitarist
keyboard	keyboardist
piano	pianist
saxophone	saxophonist
trombone	trombonist
trumpet	trumpeter
violin	violinist

Review more words for people involved in music:

alto	a female singer with a low voice
bass	a male singer with a low voice
choir or chorus director	someone who directs a group of singers
conductor	someone who directs a band or an orchestra
singer	a person who makes music with his or her voice
soprano	a female singer with a high voice
tenor	a male singer with a high voice

exercise 7-5

Write the names of five musicians you like, indicating the specialty of each one.

1. _____

2. _____

3. _____

4. _____

5. _____

Words for the Arts

Music

blues: *a style of slow jazz evolved from African-American songs*
I love to listen to the **blues** when I'm lonely.

classical: *European music of the latter half of the eighteenth century; music of acknowledged excellence and serious style*
Classical music is often performed by the city's symphony orchestra.

country: *a style of popular music from the rural American south and southwest*
A lot of **country** musicians live and work in Nashville, Tennessee.

folk/ethnic: *music that originates among the common people of a region*
Folk music was very popular in the United States in the 1960s.

jazz: *a kind of music that originated with African-American bands in the southern United States, characterized by improvisation and strong, flexible rhythm*
Jazz is popular in many parts of the world.

oldies: *popular music from an earlier decade*
Her favorite **oldies** are from the 1950s and 1960s.

popular: *music that is appreciated by a large number of people during the current period of time*
That radio station plays only **popular** music.

rap: *a currently popular style of music that originated among African-American performers, characterized by talking, rather than singing, in rhyme and rhythm*
Rap is for listening, not dancing.

rhythm and blues: *a style of music with strong, simple rhythm and lyrics that originated in the late 1940s and early 1950s among African-American groups*
Rhythm and blues is great for swing dancing.

rock: *a popular style of music played by bands with electric guitars, keyboards, and drums, often with emotional singing by a group or one singer*
Rock concerts are very popular among young people.

rock and roll: *a style of music that began in the 1950s and combined elements of rhythm and blues and country*
There were a lot of TV shows with **rock-and-roll** dancers.

exercise   **7-6**

Which of these types of music do you like best? Write a few sentences to describe the music and the musicians who play it.

_____

_____

_____

Dance

ballet: *a formal, artistic dance with graceful movements and elaborate technique*
She has been dancing **ballet** since she was a child.

a ballet show
We went to the **ballet** last night.

ballroom: *a formal version of popular dance, where style and technique are important, including the* fox-trot, waltz, swing, *and* Latin, *among others*
I'm learning the waltz from my neighbor who teaches **ballroom** dancing.

dance: *movement in time with music*
Dance is a good way to exercise and relax at the same time.

an event where people go to dance
Are you going to the **dance** on Saturday night?

jazz: *a type of ballet performed to jazz music*
She is a top ballet performer and is also accomplished in **jazz**.

Latin: *any of the dances performed to popular music from Latin America, including* merengue, salsa, cumbia, bachata, mambo, samba, cha-cha, *and* tango, *among others*
He is a good swing dancer, but what he really likes is **Latin** dancing.

line: *a dance performed to country music, where dancers dance individually but all follow the same steps*
One good thing about **line** dancing is that you don't need a partner.

tap: *a dance performed with a metal plate attached to the toe or heel of the shoe*
She is good at both ballet and **tap**.

exercise 7-7

Write a sentence that tells what kind of dance you have seen or have performed.

_____

_____

Words for Places

Parks

amusement park: *a park operated as a business that has rides, games, and other entertainment*
All of the children wanted to go on the rides at the **amusement park**.

botanical garden: *a park where plants are cultivated and identified for the public*
There was a beautiful display of orchids at the **botanical garden**.

national or state park: *a parcel of land reserved by the government and administered by the government for preservation and recreation*
You can get a lot of information from the government about visiting the **national parks**.

park: *an outdoor place reserved for the pleasure of the public*
We had a picnic in the **park**.

playground: *a park set aside for children to play in, usually with swings and other equipment for them to play on*
> The kids were tired after an afternoon at the **playground**.

theme park: *an elaborate amusement park that is developed around one particular idea, such as a historical time or place, a popular character, or other special interest*
> We saw a lot of movie and TV characters at the **theme park**.

zoo: *a park where animals are kept and shown to the public*
> The children loved seeing the giraffes at the **zoo**.

exercise   7-8

Match each type of park in the left column with its description in the right column.

_____ 1. amusement park   a. a large park with people dressed in special costumes

_____ 2. botanical garden   b. a small park with swings and a sandbox

_____ 3. national park   c. a park with elephants, monkeys, lions, and tigers

_____ 4. playground   d. a park where you pay to go on rides

_____ 5. theme park   e. a large park that preserves the natural environment

_____ 6. zoo   f. a park where you can learn about different varieties of plants

Stores

boutique: *a small specialty store that sells goods carefully chosen for a particular type of customer and usually offers unique items that are not available at chain stores*
> Her sister has individual style and shops only at **boutiques**.

box store: *a large chain store that has a similar structure and layout in each location*
> If you need hardware for a project, you can go to a local hardware store or to a big **box store**.

chain store: *one of many stores owned and operated by the same company*
> With so many **chain stores**, our cities are becoming more alike.

department store: *a large store that usually has several floors, elevators and escalators, and separate departments for each type of purchase—for example, women's clothing, men's clothing, children's clothing, shoes, linens, kitchen equipment, etc.*
> It is very convenient to shop at a **department store** where you can find things for the whole family as well as household goods.

discount store: *a store that sells goods at a lower price than the one suggested by the manufacturer*
> You can save a lot of money by buying at a **discount store**, but you don't get any help in selecting your purchases.

mall store: *a chain store often located with other chain stores in a shopping mall*
> My friend loves to shop at her favorite **mall stores**.

outlet: *a store that sells goods from a particular manufacturer, at a lower price*
> **Outlets** are often grouped together in malls on the outskirts of cities.

exercise	7-9

Write the name of a store you know that fits each category listed.

1. chain store _____

2. box store _____

3. department store _____

4. discount store _____

5. outlet _____

6. mall store _____

7. boutique _____

Schools

academy: *a private school*
>He was educated at a very expensive **academy**.

college: *education beyond high school, where students take general required courses and specialize in a particular area of study leading to a bachelor's degree*
>Her mother made sure that she would be able to go to **college**.

elementary school: *a school that contains classes from kindergarten through grade five or six*
>Most children go to an **elementary school** near where they live.

graduate school: *the university programs that lead to advanced degrees, including special schools such as law school, medical school, dental school, and business school*
>Many students have full-time jobs and go to **graduate school** classes in the evening.

high school: *a school that contains classes from grades nine or ten through twelve*
>Graduation from **high school** is a requirement for admission to a college or university, and for many jobs.

kindergarten: *the first year of school, required in the United States by children aged five*
>Many children learn to read in **kindergarten**.

middle school: *a school that contains classes from grade six or seven to grade eight or nine*
>**Middle school** students are usually in the beginning stages of adolescence.

preschool: *a school for children aged three or four*
>**Preschool** is a good introduction to school for small children.

private school: *a school administered by a private organization, business, church, or other group*
>Most **private schools** require the students to wear uniforms.

public school: *a school administered by a local government where instruction is free*
>All of their children go to **public school**.

school: *a place for learning*
>He is going to open a cooking **school** in the city.

university: *a college that has four-year bachelor's degree programs and also offers graduate programs where students can do more in-depth study of a chosen subject, leading to a master's degree or a doctor's degree*

Some students prefer to get a bachelor's degree from a small college and then go to a large **university** for a master's degree.

exercise   7-10

Match each type of school with the students who would most likely attend it.

_____ 1. college   a. a three-year-old child

_____ 2. elementary school   b. a nine-year-old child

_____ 3. graduate school   c. the majority of children in the United States

_____ 4. high school   d. a five-year-old child

_____ 5. kindergarten   e. a twelve-year-old child

_____ 6. language school   f. a sixteen-year-old

_____ 7. middle school   g. a person who wants to continue to study after high school

_____ 8. preschool   h. a person who wants to continue to study after college

_____ 9. public school   j. a person who wants to learn French

Words for Things

Houses

apartment: *a place to live that is part of a larger building, owned by a landlord who collects monthly rent*
They will rent an **apartment** until they have enough money to buy a house.

cabin: *a small, roughly built house*
The family likes to stay in a **cabin** in the mountains in the summer.

a bedroom on a ship
The **cabins** on the ship are quite small.

an inside area of an airplane
Those airplanes have a very large passenger **cabin**.

condominium: *a building or group of buildings whose apartments are individually owned*
They are building a new **condominium** near here.

an apartment in a condominium
As soon as he graduated he bought a **condominium** in the city.

cottage: *a small house of one story*
His family has a **cottage** at the beach, where they go every summer.

house: *a building designed as a place to live*
> They are expecting a baby and want to move to a bigger **house**.

hut: *a small shelter, with no amenities*
> The children made a **hut** in the woods.

mansion: *a large house*
> The mayor's official residence is a beautiful **mansion**.

rambler: *a house, bigger than a cottage, that has a number of rooms that are all on one floor.*
> They are looking for a **rambler**, because her mother can't climb steps.

townhouse: *a house built in a row of houses, with side walls connected*
> **Townhouses** usually have a lot of steps.

exercise 7-11

Match each type of home in the column on the left with its description from the column on the right.

_____ 1. hut

a. one bedroom, one bath, living room, dining room, kitchen, in a large building of similar units all owned by a company

_____ 2. cabin

b. one bedroom, one bath, living room, dining room, kitchen, in a large building of similar units each individually owned

_____ 3. condominium

c. living room, dining room, kitchen on main level, two bedrooms and bath on second level, one bedroom and bath on third level, recreation room in basement, in row of similar houses

_____ 4. cottage

d. seven bedrooms, eight bathrooms, twelve-foot ceilings, ballroom, swimming pool, guest house, on two landscaped acres

_____ 5. apartment

e. one room, mud floor, low ceiling

_____ 6. mansion

f. bedroom–living room combination, kitchen, outdoor shower, toilet in outhouse

_____ 7. rambler

g. five bedrooms, four bathrooms, living room, dining room, kitchen, all on one floor

_____ 8. townhouse

h. two bedrooms, kitchen–dining room combination, living room, one bath, all on one floor, pretty rose garden and white picket fence

Streets

avenue: *a wide street in a city*
> The **avenues** in the city are wide and elegant.

beltway: *a freeway that forms a circle around a city, connecting its outer suburbs*
> Traffic is fast on the **beltway**, and you have to be careful.

freeway: *a highway with several lanes and few or no stoplights; vehicles enter and exit via ramps*
> There are always a lot of trucks on the **freeway**.

highway: *a main public road that connects towns and cities*
  The **highway** is usually crowded.

road: *an open way for the passage of vehicles, people, or animals*
  The **road** that leads to our cabin is not paved.

street: *a public way for automobiles, usually with buildings on both sides*
  What **street** do you live on?

toll road: *a freeway that charges money to use it*
  We took the **toll road** and got there much faster, but it cost ten dollars in tolls.

 **exercise   7-12**

Write the names or route numbers of examples of each type of street.

1. street   _____

2. road   _____

3. avenue   _____

4. highway   _____

5. freeway   _____

6. toll road   _____

7. beltway   _____

Automobiles

automobile: *a passenger vehicle that has four wheels and its own engine, for travel on land*
  Many families have more than one **automobile**.

car: *an automobile*
  Our neighbors just bought a new **car**.

convertible: *a car whose top can be folded back or removed*
  It's very pleasant to ride in a **convertible** in nice weather.

sedan: *a car that has a front seat and a rear seat and either two doors or four doors*
  The **sedan** is a popular car style.

SUV: *(Sport Utility Vehicle) a high-performance four-wheel-drive car built on a truck frame*
  There are lots of **SUVs** on the streets, especially in the suburbs.

van: *a large boxlike automobile that has sliding side doors*
  Many people who have small children buy either an SUV or a **van**.

vehicle: *any device used for carrying passengers, goods, or equipment*
  Bicycles, motorcycles, cars, and sleds are all **vehicles**.

exercise	7-13

Observe on the street examples of each type of vehicle listed, and make a note of the name of each one. Write a description of the color and make of each one.

1. sedan _____

2. convertible _____

3. SUV _____

4. van _____

Shoes

boots: *a protective covering for the feet and part of the legs*
You need **boots** for walking in the snow.

flats: *women's shoes that have a very low heel*
Flats are more comfortable for walking.

high heels: *women's shoes that have a built-up heel, often three to four inches high*
Many women like to get dressed up in **high heels**.

lace-ups: *shoes that are tightened to the feet by laces that are threaded through holes in the upper part of the shoe*
Children usually get their first **lace-ups** when they are learning to walk.

loafers: *men's or women's slip-on leather shoes that look like moccasins with a solid sole*
Loafers are more casual than oxfords, but they are dressier than sneakers.

Mary Janes: *little girls' shoes with a strap over the top*
Even big girls and women like **Mary Janes**.

moccasins: *soft leather shoes traditionally worn by native North Americans*
Mocassins are especially pretty when they have decorative beading.

oxfords: *leather lace-ups*
Some private schools require the students to wear **oxfords** as part of the school uniform.

pumps: *women's medium-heel or high-heel shoes with closed toe*
Pumps can be worn almost anywhere.

sandals: *shoes made of a sole and straps*
Sandals are great in the summertime.

shoes: *a covering for a person's feet*
Everybody likes to get new **shoes**.

sneakers: *sports shoes with rubber soles; tennis shoes, running shoes, basketball shoes, etc.*
People of all ages wear **sneakers**.

wedges: *high heels with a solid portion that connects the heels to the sole*
Wedges seem to go in and out of style.

exercise   **7-14**

During the next week, look at the shoes of people on the street for examples of each type of shoe on the list, and make a note that describes each type and the person who is wearing it. Write your descriptions here.

1. sandals _____

2. boots _____

3. high heels _____

4. flats _____

5. wedges _____

6. pumps _____

7. Mary Janes _____

8. loafers _____

9. lace-ups _____

10. oxfords _____

11. sneakers _____

Words for Events

Parties

brunch: *a party where both breakfast and lunch dishes are served*
   Brunches are popular on Sunday mornings.

cocktail party: *a large party where drinks and snacks are served and where guests stand up and move around to talk to other guests*
   Cocktail parties are good places to meet new people.

dinner party: *a party where a formal evening meal is served*
   She has very elegant **dinner parties** and always invites interesting people.

engagement party: *a party to congratulate a couple on their commitment to marry one another*
   Her sister is having an **engagement party** for them.

get-together: *an informal party*
   Our group of friends has a **get-together** every month or so.

luncheon: *a party where a formal lunch is served*
   Her mother invited all of the wedding party to a **luncheon**.

open house: *a large party where the guests may arrive and leave at any time during the suggested hours*
   We were invited to an **open house** on New Year's Day.

party: *a group of people meeting together for the purpose of having fun*
> I'm always ready for a **party**.

> *a group of people who do something together*
> The restaurant is reserving a table for a **party** of six people.

reception: *a party to meet, welcome, or say good-bye to someone*
> The company invited me to a **reception** to meet the new vice president.

shower: *a party where the guests bring gifts for a bride-to-be or mother-to-be*
> Our office is planning a **shower** for our assistant, who is expecting a baby in January.

wedding: *a ceremony to celebrate a marriage*
> Were you invited to the **wedding**?

exercise 7-15

Write a few sentences telling what kind of party you like to attend and why you like that kind of party.

_____

_____

_____

_____

Shows

comedy: *a play designed to make people laugh*
> The play was a **comedy** about the humor in family life.

concert: *a music show*
> The university students were excited about the **concert** given by their favorite band.

drama: *a serious play*
> The play was a **drama** about serious issues in family life.

fashion show: *a show where models wear the latest fashions to introduce them to the public*
> It's exciting to see the **fashion shows** in New York, Milan, and Paris.

game show: *a television show where people play games to win money or prizes*
> She was on that **game show** and won a new car.

movie: *a motion picture or film*
> What **movies** are playing in our neighborhood?

opera: *a play set to music*
> We went to the **opera** when we were in Italy.

play: *a story written to be acted on a stage*
> The high school seniors put on a **play** at the end of the year.

reality show: *a television show that films people as they live their own lives*
>   A **reality show** can be funny or sad.

show: *an exhibition or entertainment for the public*
>   The movie was an excellent **show**.

soap opera: *a TV show that shows daily episodes of a story that never ends*
>   If you start watching a **soap opera**, it is hard to stop.

TV show: *a show broadcast on television*
>   He doesn't want to stay home and watch **TV shows**.

exercise	7-16

Write a few sentences that name and describe a show you have seen recently.

_____

_____

_____

_____

_____

Games

board game: *a game played on a flat board specially designed for it, often with small pieces that belong to each player, and dice*
>   **Board games** are fun for children and adults.

card game: *a game played with a standard deck of cards or cards specially designed for it; bridge, canasta, hearts, Old Maid, Go Fish, etc.*
>   There are **card games** for children and for adults.

game: *an entertainment where two or more people compete with each other*
>   Would you like to play a **game** with me?

hide-and-seek: *a children's game where one child, who is "it," must find another child in his or her hiding place, who then becomes "it"*
>   **Hide-and-seek** is a game played everywhere.

match: *a tennis, soccer, or rugby game*
>   I'd love to go to the movies, but I have a tennis **match** this afternoon.

parlor game: *an indoor game that is played among small groups of people at a party*
>   Charades is a popular **parlor game**.

sports: *an athletic competition; a football game, a baseball game, a volleyball game, etc.*
>   He loves to spend Sundays watching **sports**.

tag: *a children's game where one child, who is "it," must touch (tag) another, who then becomes "it"*
>   **Tag** is a game played by children of all ages.

exercise	7-17

Match each type of game in the left column with one of the descriptions in the right column.

_____ 1. baseball game

a. four players sit around a table; one of them distributes a number of cards to all of the players; players try to win other players' cards, according to a set of rules

_____ 2. board game

b. two players stand on opposite sides of a net and hit a ball back and forth over the net with a racket; a score is made when a player cannot return the ball

_____ 3. card game

c. two teams of nine players each; players hit balls pitched to them by the other team, then try to run around three bases and then to home plate, where a score is made

_____ 4. children's game

d. three or four players arrange their pieces on a board and roll dice to see how many steps they can take in their goal of getting around the board first

_____ 5. parlor game

e. a number of children stand in a circle, while the child who is "it" drops a handkerchief behind one of them; that child then runs after the first one, tags him or her, and becomes "it"

_____ 6. tennis match

f. the guests at a party are divided into teams; one member of each team tries to help his or her teammates guess the answer to a problem, but with restrictions set by the rules of the game

Storms

cyclone: *a violent storm with rotating wind*
They changed their vacation plans because of the **cyclone** warning.

gale: *a wind with a speed between thirty-two and sixty-three miles per hour (between fifty and one hundred kilometers per hour)*
We'd better stay home. It looks like a **gale** outside.

hurricane: *a tropical storm with winds of seventy-four miles per hour (119 kilometers per hour) or greater*
The **hurricane** took the roof off our neighbor's house.

sandstorm: *a storm of sand in the desert*
During the **sandstorm** there were clouds of sand in the air.

storm: *a strong wind with rain, snow, or hail, and sometimes with thunder and lightning*
They had to stop driving because of the **storm**.

tornado: *a violent storm that whirls in a circular motion at speeds up to three hundred miles per hour*
Everyone must seek shelter; there is a **tornado** warning for the area.

exercise	7-18

Replace each italicized word with a more descriptive one.

1. There was a *storm* with winds of eighty miles an hour. _____

2. We stayed in from the *storm* because the winds were blowing at fifty miles an hour.

   _____

3. There was a violent *storm* in the desert. _____

4. The *storm* whirled around at 250 miles per hour, destroying everything.

   _____

PART II

ADJECTIVES

Adjectives are the words that allow us to be artists. Instead of painting the colors or making the music, we can use adjectives—*red, beautiful, lively, loud*—to describe the nouns in our lives.

Adjectives can be simple to use, as they don't change to fit the nouns they describe. For example, the same adjective can describe New York (a *big* city), New York and Los Angeles (*big* cities), or a noncount noun such as "furniture" (*big* furniture).

Adjectives can also be used to compare nouns with each other. To do this, certain adjectives have comparative and superlative forms that are made by adding *-er* or *-est* at the end, for example, "He is *taller* than his brother" or "He is the *tallest* boy in the class." Others are preceded by *more* or *most* to make these comparisons, for example, "She is *more patient* than the other teacher" or "She is the *most patient* teacher at the school."

When you know the patterns for using adjectives, it is easy to add new ones to your vocabulary. Enjoy adjectives and be creative!

Making Descriptions

Adjectives describe nouns and are usually placed before the nouns they describe:

> This is **good** food.
>
> He's a **nice** man.
>
> She has an **expensive** car.
>
> I got **cheap** tickets.

A form of the verb *be* can separate an adjective from the noun (or pronoun) it describes:

> The food is **good**.
>
> That man is **nice**.
>
> Her car is **expensive**.
>
> The tickets were **cheap**.

Two adjectives can be connected by the word *and*:

> Her car is **big** and **expensive**.
>
> The man is **smart** and **nice**.

A comma is used to separate adjectives when there are more than two:

> Her car is **big**, **comfortable**, and **expensive**.
>
> The man is **smart**, **nice**, and **handsome**.

Adjectives That Describe People

Adjectives describe a person's physical and personal characteristics. They answer the questions, "What are you like?" "What is she like?" "What is he like?" and "What are they like?" Review the words in the following list:

able	good	responsible
aggressive	handsome	rich
beautiful	interesting	silly
big	large	smart
brave	lazy	strict
charming	mean	sweet
fast	nice	tall
fat	old	unhappy
friendly	pretty	weak
funny	proud	
generous	quiet	

 **exercise**   **8-1**

Fill in each blank with one or several words from the list.

1. I am _____.

2. My neighbors are _____.

3. A friend of mine is _____.

4. I don't know anyone who is _____.

5. Most of the people I see every day are _____.

Antonyms

Antonyms are two words with opposite meanings. The adjectives in the following exercises are antonyms of the adjectives in the previous list, but not in the same order.

 **exercise**   **8-2**

Fill in the antonym for each adjective using the list provided.

cowardly   handicapped   little   shy   slow   stingy   thin   ugly   unfriendly

1. able   _____

2. aggressive   _____

3. big   _____

4. brave   _____

5. beautiful   _____

6. fast   _____

7. fat _____

8. friendly _____

9. generous _____

exercise | 8-3

Fill in the antonym for each adjective using the list provided.

bad boring energetic humble kind noisy plain small young

1. good _____

2. interesting _____

3. large _____

4. lazy _____

5. mean _____

6. old _____

7. pretty _____

8. proud _____

9. quiet _____

exercise | 8-4

Fill in the antonym for each adjective using the list provided.

bitter dumb easygoing happy poor serious short strong

1. rich _____

2. silly _____

3. smart _____

4. strict _____

5. sweet _____

6. tall _____

7. unhappy _____

8. weak _____

Prefixes

Many antonyms can be formed by adding a *prefix* to an adjective. The prefixes *in-*, *im-*, *ir-*, and *un-* all mean "not."

exercise   8-5

Fill in the antonym for each adjective using the prefixes indicated.

in-

    EXAMPLE: active   *inactive*

1. capable   _____

2. competent   _____

3. considerate   _____

4. efficient   _____

5. secure   _____

6. sincere   _____

7. tolerant   _____

   im-

    EXAMPLE: mature   *immature*

8. modest   _____

9. patient   _____

10. polite   _____

11. proper   _____

   ir-

    EXAMPLE: responsible   *irresponsible*

12. resistible   _____

13. reverent   _____

   un-

    EXAMPLE: friendly   *unfriendly*

14. balanced   _____

15. civil   _____

16. civilized _____

17. disciplined _____

18. enthusiastic _____

19. faithful _____

20. fortunate _____

21. happy _____

22. healthy _____

23. kind _____

24. natural _____

25. pleasant _____

26. popular _____

27. reasonable _____

28. selfish _____

29. successful _____

30. tidy _____

31. trustworthy _____

32. truthful _____

Suffixes

Some adjectives are formed by adding a *suffix* to a noun:

-ful

care	careful
cheer	cheerful
harm	harmful
skill	skillful
tact	tactful
success	successful
truth	truthful

Some (but not all) adjectives that end in *-ful* have antonyms that end in *-less*:

careful	**careless**
harmful	**harmless**
tactful	**tactless**

exercise   8-6

Write in the antonyms for the adjectives indicated. (Be careful—some of these are tricky!)

EXAMPLE: beautiful   *ugly*

1. careful   _____

2. faithful   _____

3. harmful   _____

4. successful   _____

5. tactful   _____

6. truthful   _____

The following are also adjective suffixes: *-ent, -able, -ible, -ic, -ly,* and *-ive.* Review the adjectives in the following chart:

-ent	*-able*	*-ible*	*-ic*	*-ly*	*-ive*
independent	adorable	flexible	athletic	cowardly	aggressive
insistent	hospitable	gullible	idealistic	friendly	appreciative
intelligent	likable	responsible	materialistic	lively	creative
persistent			optimistic	lonely	imaginative
			pessimistic	lovely	manipulative
					persuasive

exercise   8-7

Fill in each blank with the best word from the prefix group indicated.

-ent

1. A person who is smart is _____.

2. Someone who *persists* doesn't stop trying; that person is _____.

3. Someone who succeeds alone, who doesn't *depend* on help from others, is

   _____.

4. People who demand action, or *insist* on it, are _____.

-able/-ible

5. People who welcome you to their home are _____.

6. A person who is pleasant, kind, helpful, and friendly is _____.

7. Someone who does his work well and on time is _____ .

8. Babies are cute; when they smile they are _____ .

9. A person who believes ridiculous stories is _____ .

10. People who can adapt to others' needs are _____ .

-ic

11. People who expect a good future are _____ .

12. People who expect a bad future are _____ .

13. A person who is good at sports, such as tennis or football, is _____ .

14. Someone who needs to own expensive things is _____ .

15. A person who believes the future will be almost perfect is _____ .

-ly

16. A person who has a beautiful personality is _____ .

17. Someone who has a lot of energy and enthusiasm is _____ .

18. People who are afraid to act are _____ .

19. A person who likes to talk to and help others is _____ .

20. A person who has no friends is probably _____ .

-ive

21. *Creative* people have new ideas; they are _____ .

22. A person who likes to control the actions of others is _____ .

23. A person who gets other people to form an opinion is _____ .

24. People who demand to be first are _____ .

25. A person who is thankful is _____ .

Using Adjectives with Other Words

A/an, the, this, that, these, those, my, your, his, her, our, and *their* are *determiners.* An adjective goes between the determiner and the noun it describes:

the irresponsible student
those aggressive lawyers
my adorable friend
our athletic neighbor

The word *a* goes before an adjective that begins with a consonant sound; *an* goes before an adjective that begins with a vowel sound:

      a creative child
      an independent woman

exercise 8-8

Write a *or* an *in the blank before each adjective.*

1. He is _____ good friend.

2. She is _____ interesting girl.

3. My coworker is _____ optimistic person.

4. Her doctor is _____ capable surgeon.

5. That politician is _____ aggressive leader.

exercise 8-9

Use at least ten adjectives from this unit to describe yourself and other people you know. Be sure to write complete sentences.

1. _____

2. _____

3. _____

4. _____

5. _____

6. _____

7. _____

8. _____

9. _____

10. _____

Proper Adjectives

Proper adjectives describe people or things by their place of origin or group association. Proper adjectives are written with a capital letter:

African	European
African-American	Jewish
Asian	Mexican
Australian	Muslim
Buddhist	Native American
Canadian	North American
Caribbean	Japanese
Central American	South American
Christian	Western

exercise 8-10

Fill in the blanks with the appropriate proper adjectives.

1. Most of the people who live in my neighborhood are _____.

2. I work with a lot of _____ people.

3. I know only a few _____ people.

4. _____ music is my favorite.

5. _____ food is delicious.

Adjectives That Describe a Person's Condition

Adjectives describe a person's condition. They answer the questions, "How are you?" "How is she?" "How is he?" and "How are they?" Review the words in the following list:

busy	happy	so-so
calm	hungry	thirsty
cold	lost	tired
confused	nervous	upset
dead	ready	warm
dirty	satisfied	worried
fine	scared	
glad	sick	

exercise   8-11

Circle the word that best fills in each blank.

1. I had to eat something because I was so _____.

   worried   **hungry**   **thirsty**   **calm**

2. I didn't call you because I knew you were _____.

   busy   **so-so**   **dead**   **glad**

3. We are leaving at 6:00 tomorrow morning. Please be _____.

   worried   **scared**   **lost**   **ready**

4. If you are _____, get a drink from the refrigerator.

   satisfied   **confused**   **thirsty**   **dirty**

5. We're sorry you are _____ and hope you feel better soon.

   happy   **upset**   **glad**   **fine**

6. If you are too _____, put on a sweater.

   cold   **warm**   **tired**   **nervous**

Antonyms

Review the adjectives in the following list:

alive
anxious/upset/nervous
clean
cool
dissatisfied
full
hot
rested
sad/depressed
well

exercise   8-12

Find in the previous list the antonym for each of the following adjectives.

1. calm _____

2. cold _____

3. dead _____

4. dirty _____

5. happy _____

6. hungry _____

7. satisfied _____

8. sick _____

9. tired _____

10. warm _____

The conjunction *but* between adjectives indicates contrast.

> I'm **fine** but **tired**.
> She is **sick** but **comfortable**.
> They are **hungry** but **happy**.
> We're **nervous** but **ready**.

exercise   8-13

Answer each question in complete sentences, using at least ten different adjectives. Connect two adjectives with and *or* but. *Use commas when you have more than two adjectives together.*

1. How are you today? _____

_____

2. How is your best friend? _____

_____

3. How is everyone in your family? _____

_____

Adjectives That Describe Objects

Size

Review the following adjectives that describe things by their size:

little/small	medium-sized	big/large
tiny	average-sized	huge/enormous
narrow	of medium width	wide
short	of medium length	long
light	of medium weight	heavy

exercise   8-14

Write the antonyms for the following.

1. wide   _____

2. little   _____

3. heavy   _____

4. enormous   _____

5. long   _____

exercise   8-15

Describe by size five objects that you see right now. Be sure to write in complete sentences.

1. _____

2. _____

3. _____

4. _____

5. _____

Shape

Review the following adjectives that describe things by their shape:

diamond-shaped
rectangular
round
square
triangular

exercise 8-16

Answer each question in a complete sentence.

1. What do you see that is round?

   _____

2. What do you have that is square?

   _____

3. What traffic sign is triangular?

   _____

4. What is the shape of this book?

   _____

5. What is the shape of a baseball field?

   _____

Color

Review the following adjectives that describe things by their color:

black	green	pink	yellow
blue	gray	purple	white
brown	orange	red	

A color mixed with white is called "light": light blue, light green. A color mixed with black is called "dark": dark red, dark purple. Fashion colors are often named after flowers, fruit, or other natural items: rose, lilac, turquoise, tomato, avocado, chocolate, bark.

exercise 8-17

Describe five things you see by their color. Use complete sentences.

1. _____

2. _____

3. _____

4. _____

5. _____

Quality

Review the following adjectives that describe things by their quality:

acceptable	inefficient
cheap	inferior
comfortable	shoddy
convenient	special
cozy	sturdy
delicious	superior
effective	terrible
efficient	unacceptable
excellent	uncomfortable
expensive	unimportant
favorite	useful
inconvenient	useless
inedible	well-made
incffective	wobbly

exercise   8-18

Match the adjectives in the left column with their antonyms in the right column.

_____ 1. acceptable	a. expensive
_____ 2. cheap	b. inconvenient
_____ 3. comfortable	c. inedible
_____ 4. convenient	d. ineffective
_____ 5. delicious	e. inferior
_____ 6. effective	f. shoddy
_____ 7. excellent	g. terrible
_____ 8. special	h. unacccptable
_____ 9. sturdy	i. uncomfortable
_____ 10. superior	j. unimportant
_____ 11. useful	k. useless
_____ 12. well-made	l. wobbly

Condition

Review the following adjectives that describe things by their condition:

broken	neat
clean	new
dirty	old
dusty	patched
empty	ragged
fixed	ruined
fresh	spoiled/rotten
full	tidy
like-new	torn
messy	worn

exercise 8-19

Write the antonym to each of the following adjectives.

1. full _____

2. old _____

3. torn _____

4. neat _____

5. clean _____

6. fixed _____

7. rotten _____

exercise 8-20

Describe the condition of five things you have.

1. _____

2. _____

3. _____

4. _____

5. _____

Adjectives That Describe Places

Review the following adjectives that describe places:

airy	light
badly designed	modern
badly located	old-fashioned
cheap	open
cramped	private
crowded	rundown
damp	safe
dangerous	spacious
dark	unfurnished
dry	well-built
empty	well-designed
expensive	well-located
furnished	well-maintained

exercise   8-21

Find the antonyms to the following adjectives in the previous list, and write them in the blanks:

1. cheap _____

2. cramped _____

3. crowded _____

4. damp _____

5. dangerous _____

6. dark _____

7. furnished _____

8. rundown _____

9. private _____

10. modern _____

exercise   8-22

Use at least ten adjectives from the previous list to describe the place you are in right now.

1. _____

2. _____

3. _____

4. _____

5. _____

6. _____

7. _____

8. _____

9. _____

10. _____

Adjectives That Describe the Weather

Review the adjectives in the following list:

breezy	humid
chilly	icy
clear	nice
cloudy	pleasant
cold	rainy
cool	stormy
dry	sunny
foggy	unpleasant
freezing	warm
hot	windy

exercise	8-23

Complete the following chart by listing the adjectives that describe pleasant weather and those that describe unpleasant weather.

Pleasant Weather	**Unpleasant Weather**
_____	_____
_____	_____
_____	_____
_____	_____
_____	_____
_____	_____
_____	_____
_____	_____

exercise	8-24

Fill in the blanks with the most appropriate words from the previous list.

1. I don't like to go out on a(n) _____ day.

2. In January the weather is often _____.

3. In May it is usually _____ where I live.

4. Today where I live it is _____.

5. People often go swimming when it is _____.

6. It is dangerous to drive when it is _____.

7. It's good to have an umbrella on a _____ day.

8. It's a good idea to wear a hat when it is _____.

9. A hat can blow off if it is _____.

10. You need a light jacket when it is _____.

Comparisons and Superlatives

Making an Adjective Stronger or Weaker

Review the following chart:

not at all < not very < a little < somewhat < rather < pretty < very < extremely

not at all = The adjective mentioned does not describe the noun.

The tickets are **not at all** cheap.

not very — The noun does not have much of the quality of the adjective.

That area is **not very** safe.

a little = The noun has only a little bit of the quality of the adjective.

The car is **a little** expensive.

somewhat = The noun has some of the quality of the adjective.

The food is **somewhat** spicy.

rather = The noun has quite a few aspects of the quality of the adjective.

It's a **rather** large class.

pretty = The noun has a lot of the quality of the adjective.

It's a **pretty** long trip.

very = The noun is a good example of the quality of the adjective.

They're **very** good books.

extremely   =   The noun is a superior example of the quality of the adjective.

It's an **extremely** hard course.

| **exercise** | 9-1 |

Fill in the blanks with the word from the previous list that best completes each sentence.

1. My sister's job is to feed the neighbor's cats. Her job is _____ easy.

2. My friend bought a car for $100. His car was _____ expensive.

3. Our neighbor has a dog that barks all night. Our neighbor's dog is

   _____ noisy.

4. Their house is near the metro station and the bus stop. Their house is in a

   _____ convenient location.

5. She invited about fifty people to her house for a celebration. She had a

   _____ large party.

| **exercise** | 9-2 |

Now complete the following sentences with the same types of expressions.

1. My job is _____ easy.

2. My shoes were _____ expensive.

3. My neighbor's dog is _____ friendly.

4. My house is in a _____ convenient location.

5. My dinner last night was _____ salty.

Expressing Negative Effects

The word *too* before an adjective indicates that the adjective is so strong that it has a negative effect:

That car is **too expensive**. (I can't buy it.)
He is **too rich**. (He values money over people.)
They were **too tired**. (They couldn't work.)
The party was **too noisy**. (The police came and sent everybody home.)

exercise 9-3

After each sentence with too, *write a possible negative effect.*

1. The food was too cold. _____

2. It was too rainy. _____

3. I ate too much cake. _____

4. She was driving too fast. _____

5. The shoes are too small. _____

exercise 9-4

Write five sentences that describe yourself or people you know. Use five of these expressions: not at all, a little, somewhat, rather, pretty, very, extremely, too.

1. _____

2. _____

3. _____

4. _____

5. _____

Making Comparisons with Adjectives

Nouns are compared with other nouns by the strength of their adjectives. An adjective made stronger is followed by the word *than* in a comparison.

One-Syllable Adjectives

Adjectives that have only one syllable are made stronger by adding the suffix *-er*:

She is **taller than** her sister.
He is **faster than** the other runner.
These tickets were **cheaper than** those.
It is **colder** in the north **than** in the south.

exercise   9-5

Write the stronger form of each of the following adjectives.

1. bright   _____

2. cheap   _____

3. clean   _____

4. cold   _____

5. cool   _____

6. damp   _____

7. dark   _____

8. fast   _____

9. fresh   _____

10. high   _____

11. light   _____

12. long   _____

13. neat   _____

14. new   _____

15. old   _____

16. plain   _____

17. poor   _____

18. rich   _____

19. short   _____

20. sick   _____

21. slow   _____

22. small   _____

23. smart   _____

24. sweet _____

25. tall _____

26. young _____

Adjectives that have one syllable and that end in *-e* are made stronger by adding *-r*:

He is **nicer than** his brother.
They are **cuter than** they were before.

exercise 9-6

Write the stronger form of each of the following adjectives.

1. cute _____

2. fine _____

3. lame _____

4. loose _____

5. nice _____

6. pale _____

7. rude _____

8. tame _____

9. wide _____

A few one-syllable adjectives end in *-w*, *-x*, or *-y*. These are made stronger by adding *-er*:

low   **lower**
new   **newer**
slow   **slower**
lax   **laxer**
gray   **grayer**

Other adjectives of one syllable that end in a consonant-vowel-consonant are made stronger by repeating the final consonant and adding *-er*:

She is **bigger** than he is.
I think she's **thinner** than she was before.

exercise   9-7

Write the stronger form of each of the following adjectives.

1. big   _____

2. fat   _____

3. fit   _____

4. hot   _____

5. mad   _____

6. red   _____

7. sad   _____

8. thin   _____

The comparative (stronger) forms of *good* and *bad* are irregular:

> That was a **good** movie, but this one is **better**.
> She had **bad** luck, and now it is **worse**.

exercise   9-8

Use good, bad, better, *or* worse *to complete the sentences.*

1. Today's weather is _____. Yesterday's was _____.

2. The job I have is _____. It is _____ than the one I had before.

3. The condition of my room is _____. It is _____ than it was last week.

4. Today I feel _____. I feel _____ than I did yesterday.

Two-Syllable Adjectives

A lot of adjectives have two syllables and end in *-y*. They are made stronger by changing the *y* to *i* and adding *-er*:

> He is **happier** now.
> I hope it will be **sunnier** tomorrow.
> That movie is **funnier** than the last one we saw.

exercise   **9-9**

Write the stronger form of each of the following adjectives.

1. angry   _____

2. bossy   _____

3. busy   _____

4. cloudy   _____

5. cozy   _____

6. crazy   _____

7. dirty   _____

8. easy   _____

9. friendly   _____

10. funny   _____

11. happy   _____

12. lazy   _____

13. lonely   _____

14. lovely   _____

15. lucky   _____

16. noisy   _____

17. pretty   _____

18. rainy   _____

19. silly   _____

20. sunny   _____

21. tasty   _____

22. ugly   _____

A few adjectives that have two syllables are made stronger by adding -r (if they end in -e) or -er:

cruel   **crueler**
gentle   **gentler**
little   **littler**
narrow   **narrower**
quiet   **quieter**
simple   **simpler**

This street is **narrower** than that one.
This exercise is **simpler** than the other one.

exercise   9-10

Fill in each blank with the comparative form of the best adjective from the previous list.

1. It was noisy last night, but now it is _____.

2. The last problem was complicated. This one is _____.

3. The streets in that town are _____ than the avenues in the city.

4. At first he was too rough with the puppy, but now he is _____.

5. The first king was cruel, and this one is _____.

6. This little girl has a baby sister who is _____ than she is.

Most adjectives that have two or more syllables are made stronger by placing the word *more* before them:

more modern   **more** wonderful   **more** responsible
more famous   **more** dangerous   **more** imaginative

exercise   9-11

Write the comparative form of each adjective. Some will end in -er; others will have more *before them.*

1. athletic   _____

2. boring   _____

3. civil   _____

4. civilized   _____

5. clean   _____

6. comfortable   _____

7. considerate   _____

8. cool   _____

9. delicious   _____

10. dirty   _____

11. fresh   _____

12. friendly   _____

13. gentle   _____

14. gullible   _____

15. healthy   _____

16. hot   _____

17. open   _____

18. patient   _____

19. persuasive   _____

20. pleasant   _____

21. proper   _____

22. proud   _____

23. quiet   _____

24. rude   _____

25. sad   _____

26. serious   _____

27. sick   _____

28. silly   _____

29. sincere   _____

30. slow   _____

31. small   _____

32. stingy   _____

33. successful   _____

34. sweet   _____

35. tiny   _____

36. unfriendly   _____

37. upset   _____

38. useful   _____

39. wide   _____

40. worried   _____

Making Adjectives Weaker

All adjectives can be made weaker by placing the words *not as* before them:

> This apple is **not as** good as the other one.
> Those dresses are **not as** pretty as these.
> These shoes are **not as** comfortable as my old ones.

In a comparison a stronger adjective is followed by *than*; a weaker adjective is followed by *as*:

> This desk is **sturdier than** that one.
> That chair is **not as comfortable as** this one.

exercise   9-12

In each blank, make the adjective in parentheses stronger or weaker, as appropriate.

1. I bought this dress because it was (pretty) _____ the others in the shop.

2. He took the shoes back to the store because they were (comfortable)

   _____ his old ones.

3. I didn't go back to that restaurant because the food was (good)

   _____ I had expected.

4. We stayed a long time at the party, because it was (good) _____ the last one.

5. The new car is nice, but it's (big) _____ the old one.

Expressing Superlatives

Superlative adjectives indicate that a noun has more of the adjective's quality than two or more other nouns:

John is five feet ten inches tall.	James is six feet tall.	Bill is six feet two inches tall.
John is tall.	James is taller than John.	Bill is taller than John and James.
		Bill is the **tallest** in the class.

Adjectives that end in *-er* in the comparative form end in *-est* in the superlative form:

bigger	**biggest**
cooler	**coolest**
nicer	**nicest**
quieter	**quietest**
sillier	**silliest**
simpler	**simplest**

The superlative forms of *good* and *bad* are irregular:

good	**best**
bad	**worst**

exercise 9-13

Write the superlative form of each adjective.

1. bad   _____

2. clean   _____

3. cold   _____

4. crazy   _____

5. cute   _____

6. friendly   _____

7. gentle   _____

8. good   _____

9. hot   _____

10. silly   _____

11. lucky   _____

12. mad   _____

13. neat   _____

14. nice   _____

15. rude   _____

16. sad   _____

 **exercise   9-14**

Choose five of the superlatives in the answers to Exercise 9-13 to describe five people you know.

1. _____

2. _____

3. _____

4. _____

5. _____

Adjectives that are preceded by *more* in their comparative form are preceded by *most* in their superlative form:

more appreciative	**most appreciative**
more difficult	**most difficult**
more modern	**most modern**
more responsible	**most responsible**

exercise   9-15

Write the superlative form of each adjective.

1. active   _____

2. bad   _____

3. cold   _____

4. comfortable   _____

5. fast   _____

6. flexible   _____

7. generous   _____

8. happy   _____

9. large   _____

10. little   _____

11. new   _____

12. noisy   _____

13. serious   _____

14. ugly   _____

15. uninteresting   _____

16. useless   _____

 **exercise**   **9-16**

Choose five of the superlatives in the answers to Exercise 9-15 to describe five people you know or things you have.

1. _____

2. _____

3. _____

4. _____

5. _____

Verbs and Nouns Used as Adjectives

Verbs Used as Adjectives

The *present participle* and the *past participle* of some verbs can be used as adjectives. The *present participle* is the form that ends in -*ing* (see also page 42):

surprise   It is **surprising** news.

excite   You have an **exciting** job.

bore   That is a **boring** program.

Review the present participles in the following list:

boring	gratifying
captivating	inspiring
caring	interesting
confusing	satisfying
daring	surprising
exciting	terrifying
fascinating	threatening
frustrating	

These adjectives describe a person or thing that "performs the action of the verb."

A **caring** mother   =   a mother who *cares for* her children.

A **boring** movie   =   a movie that *bores* the audience.

A **threatening** storm   =   a storm that *threatens* to begin soon.

exercise   10-1

Select the word that best completes each sentence:

1. We left the movie before it ended because it was _____.

   caring   **captivating**   **boring**   **exciting**

2. The math test was too hard for me; I thought the word problems were very

   _____.

   frustrating   **exciting**   **boring**   **satisfying**

3. I don't like horror movies because they are _____.

   interesting   **terrifying**   **inspiring**   **gratifying**

4. Helping other people is extremely _____.

   threatening   **confusing**   **gratifying**   **terrifying**

5. That novel has a lot of different stories happening at the same time; it is very

   _____.

   caring   **terrifying**   **surprising**   **confusing**

6. The circus trapeze artist performed a lot of dangerous stunts. He was a

   _____ young man.

   daring   **confusing**   **frustrating**   **threatening**

The *past participle* of the verb can also be used as an adjective. This is the verb form that often ends in *-ed* or *-en*. There are also quite a few irregular past participles that have different endings. (See page 144.) Following are examples of past participles that are commonly used as adjectives:

   She is **excited** about her trip.
   The toy is **broken**.
   We were **surprised** to hear the news.
   The child is **lost**.

Review the past participles in the following list:

broken	gratified	surprised
captivated	grown	terrified
closed	hidden	threatened
confused	inspired	torn
dead	interested	upset
drunk	lost	withdrawn
excited	married	worn
fascinated	satisfied	wounded
forbidden	shut	woven
forgotten	sold	written
found	spoken	
frustrated	stolen	

exercise   10-2

Choose appropriate words from the previous list to fill in the blanks.

1. She needed glasses to read the _____ words.

2. He couldn't hear the _____ words.

3. Police detectives are searching for the _____ painting.

4. It is very dangerous to drive if you are _____.

5. She lives alone now, as her children are all _____.

6. The _____ soldiers were taken to a hospital.

7. _____ fabric is sturdier than knitted fabric.

8. He used his _____ T-shirt for a rag.

9. The people could not read that book because it was on the king's list of

   _____ books.

10. Our new neighbor doesn't talk very much; she is shy and _____.

Often, the *present participle* adjective defines the *cause* of something. The *past participle* adjective defines the *person affected*:

The information was **surprising**.   We were **surprised**.
The game was **exciting**.   The fans were **excited**.
The girl is **fascinating**.   The man is **fascinated**.

exercise   10-3

Select the present participle *adjective or the* past participle *adjective, depending on which best completes each sentence.*

1. We thought the movie was **fascinating/fascinated**.

2. The children were not very **interesting/interested** in the story.

3. That is very **surprising/surprised** news.

4. I thought the questions were **confusing/confused**.

5. That movie was so scary, I was really **terrifying/terrified**.

6. When the band arrived, we were very **exciting/excited**.

7. My friend was **captivating/captivated** by that novel.

8. That store has a lot of **satisfying/satisfied** customers.

9. Waiting in line can be very **frustrating/frustrated**.

10. We were **inspiring/inspired** by our leader's speech.

Nouns Used as Adjectives

Certain nouns can be used as adjectives to tell what the noun described is made of:

a **cardboard** box   =   a box made of cardboard
a **glass** table   =   a table made of glass

exercise   10-4

Write definitions for the following items.

1. a gold necklace _____

2. a metal hook _____

3. a plastic tray _____

4. a silver bracelet _____

5. an oak floor _____

6. a wicker basket _____

7. a dirt road _____

8. a silk blouse _____

9. a wool skirt _____

10. a cotton blanket _____

Certain nouns can be used as adjectives to tell what the noun described is meant to contain. In some cases the two words are written together as one word:

| a **mailbox** | = | a box for mail |
| a **bookcase** | = | a case for books |

exercise   10-5

Write definitions for the following items.

1. a jewelry box _____

2. an ashtray _____

3. a trash can _____

4. a picture frame _____

5. a flour sack _____

6. a key ring _____

7. a grocery bag _____

8. a glove compartment _____

9. a lunchbox _____

10. a garbage pail _____

Certain nouns can be used as adjectives to tell the purpose of the noun described:

A **potato** peeler is used for peeling potatoes.
A **dishwasher** is used for washing dishes.

exercise	10-6

Write what each of the following is used for.

1. a nutcracker _____

2. a can opener _____

3. a fire extinguisher _____

4. a CD player _____

5. an ice pick _____

6. a hair dryer _____

7. nail polish remover _____

8. a pencil sharpener _____

9. spot remover _____

10. a floor polisher _____

Certain nouns can be used as adjectives to tell what is sold in the type of store described:

| a **shoe** store | – | a store where shoes are sold |
| a **grocery** store | = | a store where groceries are sold |

exercise	10-7

Write five other types of stores or shops.

1. _____

2. _____

3. _____

4. _____

5. _____

Certain nouns define other nouns by their type:

| a **motorcycle** | = | a cycle with a motor |
| **schoolwork** | = | work that is done at school |

exercise	10-8

Write the names of the items described.

1. a lock for a bicycle   _____

2. a key for a mailbox   _____

3. a garden of roses   _____

4. work that is done at home   _____

5. a desk for a student   _____

Some adjectives are formed by adding the suffix *-ed* to a noun. These adjectives often follow another descriptive adjective to which it is closed up or connected by a hyphen:

a three-**legged** stool	=	a stool with three legs
a red**headed** woodpecker	=	a woodpecker (bird) with a red head
a brown-**eyed** girl	=	a girl with brown eyes

Review the following noun + *-ed* adjectives:

evenhanded	fair, just
hardheaded	stubborn
hard-nosed	hardheaded
hotheaded	temperamental
levelheaded	sensible
long-winded	capable of giving long, boring speeches
single-minded	focused on one goal
sure-footed	cautious, secure

exercise	10-9

Circle the most appropriate adjective to fill in each blank.

1. We didn't want to do business with him because he was so _____.

   evenhanded   **hardheaded**   **sure-footed**

2. I wasn't worried on the hike because our leader was _____.

   hard-nosed   **sure-footed**   **long-winded**

3. He got the job done efficiently because of his _____ approach.

   single-minded   **long-winded**   **hotheaded**

4. The meeting went on for hours because of too many _____ speakers.

   sure-footed   **single-minded**   **long-winded**

5. The school principal treats all cases equally; she is very _____ .

   evenhanded   **single-minded**   **hard-nosed**

6. Try not to make him angry. He's so _____ he might make a scene.

   single-minded   **sure-footed**   **hotheaded**

Compound Adjectives

A noun connected to its modifiers by hyphens can be used as an adjective. The noun is used in singular form, even though it is modified by a plural marker:

a **twenty-dollar** ticket	=	a ticket that costs twenty dollars
a **ten-foot** pole	=	a pole that is ten feet long
a **two-year** lease	=	a lease that lasts two years

 **exercise 10-10**

Write definitions for the following.

1. a five-year plan _____

2. a three-year warranty _____

3. a lifetime guarantee _____

4. a ten-minute discussion _____

5. a three-pound weight _____

6. a two-week vacation _____

7. a two-year contract _____

8. an all-day meeting _____

9. an all-night party _____

10. an everyday occurrence _____

Adjective Order

When two or three adjectives are used together, they are usually in the following order:

1. quality

2. condition

3. size

4. age

5. shape

6. color

7. origin

8. material

9. type

a **beautiful old** house	(quality, age)
a **nice clean white** uniform	(quality, condition, color)
a **shiny new red** bicycle	(condition, age, color)

exercise 11-1

Rewrite the adjectives in the correct order to describe the indicated nouns.

1. skirt: silk, long, black _____

2. shoes: leather, Italian, new _____

3. earrings: silver, beautiful, Mexican _____

4. cake: birthday, rich, three-layer _____

5. mirror: heavy, antique, round _____

Describe five of your favorite things, using two or three descriptive adjectives for each one.

1. _____

2. _____

3. _____

4. _____

5. _____

PART III

VERBS

Verbs are the wonderful words that give life to language.

The most common verb, *be*, for example, allows us to tell who or what exists in the world, and also when, where, how, and why it exists. In addition, just by changing the form of the verb, we can tell about what existed in the past and what will exist in the future, plus what we wish existed or what we would do if something existed. The verb *be* is used in a different manner from all other English verbs—it has different forms and different patterns.

All other verbs follow a second set of patterns, which enable us to tell facts about people—where and how they live, what they have, how they look and feel, what they like, what they think, and what they do; they also enable us to tell how things work and what happens in the world. And again, with a change in form, we can put all this information in the past or the future, or we can make wishes and conjectures.

Verbs also enable us to ask and answer questions, give commands and suggestions, accept or refuse, and relate and communicate.

Yes, there are a lot of irregular forms that have to be memorized, but they are worth the effort. Verbs are about life. Live well with verbs!

The Verb *Be*

The most common verb is *be*. It is used to identify or describe a person or thing, or to tell its origin, state, or location.

The Present Tense of *Be*

I **am** tall.
You **are** my friend.
He **is** sick.
She **is** a smart girl.
It **is** a mistake.

We **are** at home.
You (all) **are** great helpers.
They **are** from South America.

exercise 12-1

Fill in each blank with the appropriate form of be *in the present tense.*

1. Bill _____ here.

2. Janet and Mary Jane _____ good friends.

3. Emily _____ on vacation.

4. Betty and I _____ teachers.

5. You _____ a good student.

6. I _____ not tired.

exercise   12-2

Answer each of the following questions in a complete sentence using the verb be.

1. What is your name? _____

2. Where are you from? _____

3. Who are your best friends? _____

4. Where are your best friends now? _____

5. What is in your hand? _____

6. What color is it? _____

Asking Questions with *Be*

Questions with the verb *be* are formed by reversing the subject and the verb:

I am	**Am I . . . ?**	We are	**Are we . . . ?**
You are	**Are you . . . ?**	They are	**Are they . . . ?**
He is	**Is he . . . ?**		
She is	**Is she . . . ?**		
It is	**Is it . . . ?**		

exercise   12-3

Change the following statements to questions.

1. He is here now. _____

2. You are happy. _____

3. I am sitting down. _____

4. He is asking directions. _____

5. They are building a new house. _____

6. She is turning left. _____

7. He is taking photographs. _____

8. She is riding a bicycle. _____

Making *Be* Negative

Sentences with *be* are made negative by placing **not** after the conjugated form:

I am **not** tired.	We are **not** working.
You are **not** smiling.	You all are **not** running.
He is **not** sitting in the park.	They are **not** sitting in the park.
She is **not** at home.	
It is **not** earning interest.	

Negatives are usually contracted:

I'm not	We **aren't**
You **aren't**	You (all) **aren't**
He **isn't**	They **aren't**
She **isn't**	
It **isn't**	

exercise 12-4

Make each of the sentences in Exercise 12-3 negative.

1. _____
2. _____
3. _____
4. _____
5. _____
6. _____
7. _____
8. _____

The Past Tense of *Be*

I **was** in the city.	We **were** very happy.
You **were** shy.	You (all) **were** at school.
He **was** sick.	They **were** broken.
She **was** not tired.	
It **was** good.	

exercise	12-5

Change the answers in Exercise 12-1 to the past tense.

1. _____

2. _____

3. _____

4. _____

5. _____

6. _____

exercise	12-6

Answer each question in a complete sentence using the past tense of be.

1. Where were you yesterday at 4:00? _____

2. Who was with you? _____

3. Were you indoors or outdoors? _____

4. How was the weather? _____

5. Were there other people there? _____

Non—*To Be* Verbs

Review the words in the following list that have meanings similar to *be*:

appear
become
feel
look
look like
resemble
seem
smell
sound

Regular Present Tense Forms of Verbs Other than *Be*

The basic verb is used with *I*, *you*, *we*, and *they*:

I **look** tired.   We **look** silly.

You **look** sick.   They **look** beautiful.

The basic verb + the suffix -*s* is used with *he*, *she*, and *it*:

He **looks** good.

She **looks** better.

It **looks** dirty.

| exercise | 13-1 |

Match the sentences in the left column with those in the right column.

_____ 1. She is blonde and her mother is blonde.   a. He appears angry.

_____ 2. They are smiling.   b. He looks like me.

_____ 3. You should throw it in the garbage.   c. I feel sick.

_____ 4. We need to rest.   d. It becomes boring.

_____ 5. I like the music.   e. It smells bad.

_____ 6. She is crying.   f. It sounds good.

_____ 7. His face is red.   g. She fccls sad.

_____ 8. I have brown eyes. He has brown eyes.   h. She resembles her mother.

_____ 9. It is a long book.   i. They seem happy.

_____ 10. I need to lie down.   j. We look tired.

| exercise | 13-2 |

Choose the word that best completes each sentence.

1. The music **becomes/sounds** great.

2. The girls **resemble/appear** tired.

3. We **feel/smell** tired.

4. The flowers **become/smell** wonderful.

5. He **seems/resembles** angry.

6. She **seems/resembles** her mother.

Spelling Changes in *He/She/It* Forms

The verbs *go* and *do* add *-es*:

> He **goes**.
> She **does**.

Verbs that end in *-ch* or *-sh* add *-es*:

> He **watches**.
> She **washes**.

Verbs that end in *-y* change the *y* to *i* and add *-es*:

He **cries**.
She **tries**.

The *he/she/it* form of the verb *have* is *has*:

He **has** a cold.
She **has** the flu.

exercise   13-3

Write the present tense he/she/it *forms of the following verbs.*

1. match   _____

2. eat   _____

3. have   _____

4. drink   _____

5. go   _____

6. wish   _____

7. clean   _____

8. dry   _____

9. do   _____

10. dance   _____

Regular Past Tense Forms

The past tense of most verbs is formed by adding the suffix *-ed* to the basic verb:

appear	**appeared**
look	**looked**
seem	**seemed**
sound	**sounded**

The same form is used for *I, you, he, she, it, we,* and *they*:

They **appeared** tired.
She **looked** pretty.
He **seemed** nice.
It **sounded** good.

exercise   13-4

Write the past tense forms of the following verbs.

1. clean   _____

2. open   _____

3. work   _____

4. walk   _____

5. watch   _____

Spelling Changes in Past Tense Forms

Verbs that end in *-e* add *-d*:

change   **changed**
resemble   **resembled**

One-syllable verbs that end in a vowel + a consonant repeat the consonant and add *-ed*. (Many verbs that end in a vowel + a consonant are irregular. See page 119.)

beg   **begged**
hop   **hopped**

Verbs that end in *-y* change the *y* to *i* and add *-ed*:

cry   **cried**
study   **studied**

exercise   13-5

Write the past tense forms of the following verbs.

1. stop   _____

2. close   _____

3. shop   _____

4. exercise   _____

5. try   _____

Verbs That Describe Usual Activities

Review the verbs in the following list:

brush (your teeth)	plan
call (your friends)	play
clean	rest
close (the door)	smile
comb (your hair)	talk
cook	turn (off the light)
cry	turn (on the light)
dream	walk
exercise	wash (your hands)
laugh	watch
listen	work
open (the door)	

exercise 13-6

Write the past tense form of each of the following verbs.

1. listen _____

2. laugh _____

3. turn _____

4. dream _____

5. cry _____

6. exercise _____

7. brush _____

8. smile _____

9. plan _____

10. watch _____

Telling How Often an Activity Is Performed

never < rarely/seldom < sometimes < often < a lot < every day < always

I **never** watch TV.
She **rarely** calls her friends.
Sometimes he rests in the afternoon.

We **often** play together.
You (all) laugh **a lot**.
They work **every day**.
They **always** smile.

exercise	13-7

Choose ten activities from the previous list, and write a sentence for each that tells how often you do each activity. Use the present tense.

1. _____
2. _____
3. _____
4. _____
5. _____
6. _____
7. _____
8. _____
9. _____
10. _____

More Daily Activities

Review the verbs in the following list:

come (home)	make (the bed)
drink (water)	put (on your clothes)
drive	read
eat	ride
eat/have (breakfast)	sit (down)
eat/have (dinner)	sleep
eat/have (lunch)	stand (up)
get (dressed)	take (a bath)
get (up)	take (a shower)
go (to a place)	take (off your clothes)
go (to bed)	think
lie (down)	wake (up)

exercise	13-8

Choose ten verbs from the previous list and tell how often you perform each activity. Use complete sentences.

1. _____
2. _____

3. _____

4. _____

5. _____

6. _____

7. _____

8. _____

9. _____

10. _____

Irregular Past Tense Forms

All of the verbs in the previous list have irregular past tense forms. The past tense form is listed after the slash (/):

come/came
drink/drank
drive/drove
eat/ate
get/got
go/went
lie/lay
make/made
put/put
read/read
ride/rode
sit/sat
sleep/slept
stand/stood
take/took
think/thought
wake/woke

exercise	13-9

Using verbs from the previous list in the past tense, write ten sentences that tell what you did yesterday.

1. _____

2. _____

3. _____

4. _____

5. _____

6. _____

7. _____

8. _____

9. _____

10. _____

Verbs Used for Household Activities

Review the verbs in the following list. If the past tense form is irregular, it is indicated following the slash (/):

clean (the house)
clean (up the mess)
clean (up the yard)
do (laundry)/did
do (the shopping)/did
dust (the furniture)
empty (the dishwasher)
iron (clothes)
load (the dishwasher)
make (appointments)/made
make (repairs)/made

mow (the lawn)
pay (bills)/paid
put (the groceries away)/put
scrub (floors)
sweep (the floor)/swept
take (out the trash)/took
vacuum
wash (the windows)
water (plants)
weed (the garden)

 **exercise   13-10**

Fill in the blanks using the present tense of the verbs in parentheses.

1. John (make) _____ repairs.

2. I (water) _____ the plants.

3. My friends (clean) _____ the house.

4. Mary and Jack (vacuum) _____.

5. My dad (pay) _____ the bills.

Telling When an Activity Is Performed

in the morning
in the afternoon
in the evening
in the fall
in the spring
in the summer
in the winter

at night
at 1:00
at 2:15
at 3:30
at 4:45
at 5:55
at 7:10

on Mondays
on Tuesdays
on Wednesdays
on Thursdays
on Fridays
on Saturdays
on Sundays

on holidays
on my birthday
on the first day of the month
on the tenth of June
on weekends

in January
in February
in March
in April
in May
in June
in July
in August
in September
in October
in November
in December

every day
every month
every night
every week

| **exercise** | **13-11** |

Complete each sentence by telling when the person indicated does the activity in parentheses.

1. I (rest) _____.

2. My best friend (exercise) _____.

3. My neighbors (walk) _____.

4. My friends and I (eat together) _____.

5. I (call my friends) _____.

| **exercise** | **13-12** |

Complete each sentence by telling which activities you usually perform at the times indicated.

1. On Mondays _____.

2. In the summer _____.

3. On weekends _____.

4. In the morning _____.

5. Every day _____.

| **exercise** | **13-13** |

Fill in each blank with the most appropriate verb from the list of household activities.

1. She uses a broom to _____.

2. I take the car to _____.

3. I use the iron to _____.

4. He uses the telephone to _____.

5. We use a wet rag to _____.

6. He takes out his checkbook to _____.

7. He uses a screwdriver to _____.

8. They go outside to _____.

9. We need a washer and dryer to _____.

10. I use a dry cloth to _____.

 **exercise 13-14**

Write five sentences that tell which of the activities on the household activities list you usually did when you were a child. Write the verbs in the past tense.

1. _____

2. _____

3. _____

4. _____

5. _____

Verbs Used in a Classroom

Review the verbs in the following list. Irregular past tense forms are indicated after the slash (/):

answer	play
ask (questions)	read/read
correct (mistakes)	solve (a problem)
do (exercises)/did	spell
draw (a picture)/drew	study
erase	take (a test)/took
help (someone)	take (turns)/took
learn	teach/taught
listen (to someone)	understand/understood
make (a mistake)/made	use (the computer)
pay (attention)/paid	write/wrote

exercise 13-15

Write the past tense forms of the following verbs.

1. answer _____

2. ask _____

3. correct _____

4. erase _____

5. help _____

6. learn   _____

7. listen   _____

8. pay   _____

9. play   _____

10. solve   _____

11. spell   _____

12. study   _____

13. use   _____

exercise	**13-16**

Fill in each blank with the past tense of the verb indicated.

1. My mother (teach) _____ me to read and write.

2. He (write) _____ her an e-mail last week.

3. I (understand) _____ today's lesson.

4. We (take) _____ a hard test this morning.

5. You (make) _____ only one mistake.

6. They (do) _____ all of the exercises.

7. They (draw) _____ pictures in class.

8. My friend and I (take) _____ turns with the computer.

9. She (read) _____ us a wonderful story.

10. I hope you (pay) _____ attention.

Making Verbs Negative

In the present tense, all verbs except *be* are made negative by placing *do not* or *does not* before them.

Do not is used for *I, you, we,* and *they*. It is often contracted to *don't*.

Does not is used with *he, she,* and *it*. It is often contracted to *doesn't*.

I **don't** weed the garden. We **don't** sleep late.
You **don't** rest. You (all) **don't** wake up early.
He **doesn't** exercise. They **don't** clean up the yard.
She **doesn't** smile.

exercise   **13-17**

Rewrite the following sentences, making them negative and using the contracted form.

1. He gets up at 6:00.

   _____

2. They eat breakfast together every morning.

   _____

3. She dreams during the day.

   _____

4. We buy groceries every week.

   _____

5. I laugh a lot.

   _____

In the past tense, verbs are made negative by placing *did not* before them.

Did not is often contracted to *didn't*:

I **didn't** comb my hair. We **didn't** cook.
You **didn't** wash the windows. You (all) **didn't** sweep the floor.
He **didn't** call me. They **didn't** eat dinner.
She **didn't** work.

exercise   **13-18**

Make the sentences in Exercise 13-16 negative.

1. _____

2. _____

3. _____

4. _____

5. _____

6. _____

7. _____

8. _____

9. _____

10. _____

Activities That Are Often Performed in an Office

Review the verbs in the following list. Irregular past tense forms are indicated after the slash (/):

answer (e-mail)	plan (projects)
answer (letters)	search (the Internet)
answer (the telephone)	send (a fax)/sent
attend (meetings)	take (coffee breaks)/took
check (e-mail)	type (on the keyboard)
fill (out forms)	use (the computer)
make (phone calls)/made	write (letters)/wrote
organize files	write (reports)/wrote
participate (in discussions)	

exercise   13-19

Using the verbs in the previous list, write five sentences that tell what you do or don't do at work or in an office at home. Use the present tense.

1. _____

2. _____

3. _____

4. _____

5. _____

exercise	13-20

Change the sentences in Exercise 13-19 to the past tense.

1. _____

2. _____

3. _____

4. _____

5. _____

Asking Questions

A yes-or-no question in the present tense is formed as follows:

do/does + subject + verb

Do is used with *I, you, we,* and *they*:

Do I need to do this?   **Do** we take the test today?
Do you study at night?   **Do** you (all) listen to music?
                                    Do they correct thcir work?

Does is used with *he, she,* and *it*:

Does she go to this school?
Does he correct his work?
Does the computer work?

exercise	13-21

Write yes-or-no questions in the present tense using the verbs and forms indicated. Be sure to write a question mark at the end of each question.

1. write e-mail (you) _____

2. search the Internet (he) _____

3. use the computer (she) _____

4. attend meetings (you all) _____

5. answer the telephone (thcy) _____

6. take coffee breaks (we) _____

Question Words

Review the words in the following list:

who
what
when
where
why
how
how much

An information question is formed as follows:

> **question word** + *do/does* + subject + basic verb
> **Who do** you like?
> **What does** he do?
> **When do** we take our coffee break?
> **Where do** you all go after work?
> **Why do** they have so many meetings?
> **How do** I turn on this computer?
> **How much** time **do** you have?

Questions with *who* and *what* do not use *do* if the question is about the *subject*. If the answer is the subject, it is formed as follows:

> *Who* + verb   *What* + verb
> **Who** works here?   **What** goes in this file?

exercise	13-22

Write an information question for each of the following answers. Ask the question that the italicized words answer.

1. *The telephone lists* go in that file.

   _____

2. *Mary* answers the telephone.

   _____

3. You search the Internet *in the morning.*

   _____

4. We send faxes *to the main office.*

   _____

5. They write the reports *on the computer.*

   _____

Asking Questions in the Past Tense

Yes-or-no questions in the past tense are formed as follows:

did + subject + basic verb
Did I do this correctly?
Did you fill out the forms?
Did he take the test?
Did they send you a fax?

Information questions in the past tense are formed as follows:

question word + *did* + subject + basic verb
Where did you eat lunch?
When did she go on vacation?

Questions with *who* and *what* do not use *did* if the question is about the *subject*. If the answer is the subject, it is formed as follows:

Who + verb   *What* + verb
Who wrote this letter?   **What** helped you learn?

exercise   13-23

Write a yes-or-no question for each of the following answers.

EXAMPLE: I wrote a letter today.
Did you write a letter today?

1. They took a long coffee break.

   _____

2. She didn't answer the telephone.

   _____

3. Mary wrote these e-mails.

   _____

4. I searched the Internet this afternoon.

   _____

5. John organized all my files.

   _____

exercise   13-24

Write an information question for each of the following answers. The questions should ask what the italicized words answer.

> EXAMPLES: I *wrote a letter* today.   *What did you do today?*
>
> I wrote a letter *today*.   *When did you write a letter?*

1. *I* wrote a letter today.

   _____

2. He *worked* yesterday.

   _____

3. John called me *last night*.

   _____

4. We ate *at home* on Monday night.

   _____

5. She went home *on the bus*.

   _____

Verbs Used for Shopping

Review the verbs in the following list. Irregular past tense forms are indicated after the slash (/):

ask (for advice)	read (labels)/read
ask (for help)	return
buy/bought	save (money)
cost/cost	sell/sold
examine	send/sent
find/found	show
get (a bargain)/got	sign
get (a receipt)/got	spend (money)/spent
give (money to)/gave	talk (to the manager)
hang/hung	thank (the salesclerk)
hold/held	try (on clothes)
look (at)	use (a credit card)
look (for)	wait (in line)
pay	wear/wore
pay (with cash)	write (a check)/wrote
push (a cart)	

exercise | **13-25**

Using verbs from the previous list, write five sentences that tell what you do when you shop at your favorite store.

1. _____
2. _____
3. _____
4. _____
5. _____

exercise | **13-26**

Make the sentences in Exercise 13-25 negative.

1. _____
2. _____
3. _____
4. _____
5. _____

exercise | **13-27**

Using past tense versions of the verbs from the previous list, write five sentences that tell what you did the last time you went shopping.

1. _____
2. _____
3. _____
4. _____
5. _____

exercise   13-28

Make the sentences in Exercise 13-27 negative.

1. _____

2. _____

3. _____

4. _____

5. _____

exercise   13-29

Write yes-or-no questions for the following answers. Use present tense verbs.

1. Yes, I return clothes that don't fit.

    _____

2. No, she doesn't always use her credit card.

    _____

3. Yes, she likes her new shoes.

    _____

4. No, we don't want these shirts.

    _____

5. No, he doesn't like to go shopping.

    _____

Write yes-or-no questions for the following answers. Use past tense verbs.

1. Yes, she bought a new dress.

   _____

2. Yes, he forgot to give me a receipt.

   _____

3. No, we didn't try on a lot of clothes.

   _____

4. Yes, she went shopping yesterday.

   _____

5. No, I didn't buy anything.

   _____

exercise   13-31

Write information questions for the following answers. Ask the question that the italicized words answer. (Be careful! Some sentences are in the present tense and others are in the past.)

1. *She* always gets a bargain.

   _____

2. We *waited in line* for thirty minutes.

   _____

3. They spent a lot of money *at that store*.

   _____

4. He always thanks *the salesclerk*.

   _____

5. I wrote the check *yesterday*.

_____

6. It cost *a hundred dollars*.

_____

Verbs Used in a Bank

Review the verbs in the following list. Irregular past tense forms are indicated after the slash (/):

apply (for a loan)	make (a deposit)/made
borrow (money)	make (an investment)/made
bring (documents)/brought	open (an account)
buy (a CD)/bought	order (checks)
close (an account)	pay (an installment)/paid
drive (up to the drive-up window)/drove	remember (your PIN)
earn (interest)	save (money)
forget/forgot	speak (to the loan officer)/spoke
get (a PIN)/got	transfer (funds)
get (an ATM card)/got	use (the ATM)
get (cash)/got	wait (in line)
lose/lost	withdraw (cash)/withdrew

exercise   13-32

Circle the most appropriate words to complete each sentence.

1. I had to order checks because I _____.

   earned interest   **lost my checkbook**   **got an ATM card**

2. She was in a hurry, so she _____.

   drove up to the drive-up window   **waited in line**   **ordered checks**

3. We brought cash because we wanted to _____.

   apply for a loan   **lose money**   **make a deposit**

4. I used my ATM card to _____.

   speak to the loan officer   **open an account**   **withdraw cash**

5. A good way to save money is to _____.

   order checks   **get a PIN**   **buy a CD**

exercise   13-33

Make the following sentences negative. Pay attention to the verb tenses.

1. They closed their account.

   _____

2. This account earns interest.

   _____

3. I got a new PIN.

   _____

4. He withdrew cash.

   _____

5. She makes a deposit every week.

   _____

exercise   13-34

Write a question for each of the following answers. Ask the question that the italicized words answer. Pay attention to the verb tenses.

1. *Yes*, I paid an installment last month.

   _____

2. *Yes*, we want to open an account.

   _____

3. She bought a CD *last week*.

   _____

4. He *applied for a loan*.

   _____

5. *They* withdraw cash.

   _____

exercise | 13-35 |

Write five things you did at a bank this year.

1. _____

2. _____

3. _____

4. _____

5. _____

Using the Present Progressive Tense

The present progressive tense is used to tell that an activity is being performed *now*. The following expressions are used with the present progressive tense to mean *now*:

at present
currently
this week
this month
this year

The present progressive tense is formed by conjugating *be* and adding the present participle. The present participle is the basic verb + the suffix -*ing*:

dream   **dreaming**
laugh   **laughing**

- Verbs that end in -*e* drop the *e* and add -*ing*:

dance   **dancing**
exercise   **exercising**

- Verbs that end in -*ie* change the *ie* to *y* and add -*ing*:

tie   **tying**
lie   **lying**

- Verbs that end in a vowel + consonant double the consonant and add -*ing*:

sit   **sitting**
stop   **stopping**

I **am sitting** down.   We **are watching** TV.
You **are listening** to good music.   You (all) **are making** noise.
He **is sleeping**.   They **are talking** on the phone.
She **is writing** a letter.

The present progressive tense is also used to describe an activity that is planned for the near future. The following expressions are used with the present progressive tense to tell the time of a planned activity:

at 4:00	(later) this week	on Monday	tomorrow
in August	next month	soon	tonight
later	next week	this afternoon	
(later) this month	next year	this evening	

I **am leaving** tomorrow.　　　　We **are watching** TV tonight.
You **are working** this afternoon.　You (all) **are taking** the test next week.
He **is going** home at 6:00.　　　They **are playing** the game in October.
She **is calling** him soon.

exercise   13-36

Change the following sentences from the present tense to the present progressive tense.

> EXAMPLE: I sit down.
> *I am sitting down.*

1. He cashes a check.

   _____

2. I withdraw money.

   _____

3. They open an account.

   _____

4. We apply for a loan.

   _____

5. The investment earns interest.

   _____

6. She gets cash from the ATM.

   _____

7. I save money.

   _____

8. He pays an installment on his loan.

   _____

| exercise | 13-37 |

Write five sentences that tell about activities you have planned for the coming week. Use the present progressive tense.

1. _____

2. _____

3. _____

4. _____

5. _____

Verbs Used for Outdoor Activities

Review the verbs in the following list. Irregular past tense forms are indicated after the slash (/):

ask (directions)	mail (a letter)
build/built	ride (a bicycle)/rode
buy (an ice cream)/bought	run/ran
cross (the street)	see (an accident)/saw
drive (a car)/drove	sit (in the park)/sat
get (in a car)/got	stop (in an outdoor café)
get (off the bus)/got	stroll (in the city)
get (on a bus)/got	take (a walk)/took
get (out of the car)/got	take (photographs)/took
go (jogging)/went	turn (left)
go (straight ahead)/went	turn (right)
grow (flowers)/grew	visit (the zoo)
have (a picnic)/had	wait (at a red light)
hear (airplanes)/heard	wait (at a stop sign)
lie (in the sun)/lay	work (in the garden)

| exercise | 13-38 |

Fill in each blank with an activity from the previous list that best completes the sentence.

1. I never _____.

2. My best friend always _____.

3. A lot of people where I live _____ on Sundays.

4. I like to _____ every day.

5. Sometimes in the summer my friends and I _____.

exercise	13-39

Write a question for each of the following answers. Ask the question that the italicized words answer.

1. We had a picnic *in the park.*

   _____

2. *They* get off the bus here.

   _____

3. *Yes,* he took a lot of photographs.

   _____

4. *Yes,* she lay in the sun for an hour.

   _____

5. He always buys *an ice cream.*

   _____

exercise	13-40

Make each of the following sentences negative. Use the present tense.

1. She asks directions. _____

2. We turn left here. _____

3. He drives a car. _____

4. They get lost. _____

5. I go jogging. _____

exercise	13-41

Make each of the following sentences negative. Use the past tense.

1. We saw an accident. _____

2. They had a picnic. _____

3. He got on the bus. _____

4. You turned right. _____

5. She got out of the car. _____

exercise   **13-42**

Write in the irregular past tense forms of the following verbs.

1. be _____

2. become _____

3. build _____

4. buy _____

5. come _____

6. do _____

7. draw _____

8. drink _____

9. drive _____

10. eat _____

11. feel _____

12. find _____

13. get _____

14. go _____

15. grow _____

16. have _____

17. hear _____

18. lie _____

19. make _____

20. pay _____

21. put _____

22. leave _____

23. read   _____

24. ride   _____

25. run   _____

26. see   _____

27. sit   _____

28. sleep   _____

29. spend   _____

30. stand   _____

31. sweep   _____

32. take   _____

33. teach   _____

34. think   _____

35. understand   _____

36. wake up   _____

37. withdraw   _____

38. write   _____

Verbs Used for Activities in Public Places

Review the verbs in the following list. Irregular past tense forms are indicated after the slash (/):

ask (for the check in a restaurant)
buy (something from a street vendor)/bought
drink (from a water fountain)/drank
enjoy (your meal)
enter (a building)
enter (a restaurant)
enter (a train or metro station)
get (off the elevator)/got
get (on the elevator)/got
go (through revolving doors)/went

leave (a building)/left
leave (a tip)/left
leave (the station)/left
look (at the menu)
order (your meal)
pay (the waiter)/paid
push (the button)
ride (on the escalator)/rode
talk (on your cell phone)
use (the restroom)

exercise   13-43

Change each sentence from the past tense to the present progressive tense.

1. He got off the elevator.

    _____

2. We ordered our meal.

    _____

3. She paid the waiter.

    _____

4. We left the station.

    _____

5. They went through the revolving doors.

    _____

exercise   13-44

Make the following sentences negative.

1. He is leaving the building.

    _____

2. She is enjoying her meal.

    _____

3. They are riding on the escalator.

    _____

4. I am looking at the menu.

    _____

5. He's talking on his cell phone.

    _____

exercise   13-45

Make a question for each of the sentences in Exercise 13-44.

1. _____

2. _____

3. _____

4. _____

5. _____

Using the Present Perfect Tense

The verb *have* is used with the past participle to make the present perfect tense:

I **have**	we **have**
you **have**	you (all) **have**
he **has**	they **have**
she **has**	
it **has**	

The regular past participles are the same as the past tense forms:

cross	**crossed**
enter	**entered**
mail	**mailed**
walk	**walked**

exercise   13-46

Change the sentences in Exercise 13-40 to the present perfect tense.

1. _____

2. _____

3. _____

4. _____

5. _____

Verbs that are irregular in the past tense usually have an irregular past participle. Compare the verb forms in the following list. These are past participles of the irregular verbs you have already practiced.

Verb	Past Tense	Past Participle

PAST PARTICIPLE SAME AS THE BASIC VERB

Verb	Past Tense	Past Participle
become	became	become
come	came	come
cost	cost	cost
put	put	put
run	ran	run

PAST PARTICIPLE SAME AS THE PAST TENSE

Verb	Past Tense	Past Participle
bring	brought	brought
build	built	built
buy	bought	bought
feel	felt	felt
find	found	found
hang	hung	hung
have	had	had
hear	heard	heard
hold	held	held
leave	left	left
make	made	made
pay	paid	paid
read	read	read
sell	sold	sold
send	sent	sent
sit	sat	sat
sleep	slept	slept
spend	spent	spent
stand	stood	stood
sweep	swept	swept
teach	taught	taught
think	thought	thought
understand	understood	understood

PAST PARTICIPLE DIFFERENT FROM OTHER FORMS

Verb	Past Tense	Past Participle
be	was, were	been
do	did	done
draw	drew	drawn
drink	drank	drunk
drive	drove	driven
eat	ate	eaten
forget	forgot	forgotten
get	got	gotten
give	gave	given
go	went	gone
grow	grew	grown
lie	lay	lain
ride	rode	ridden
speak	spoke	spoken
take	took	taken
wake up	woke up	woken up
wear	wore	worn
withdraw	withdrew	withdrawn
write	wrote	written

exercise 13-47

Fill in the blank spaces with the missing forms.

Basic Verb		Past Tense		Past Participle
eat	1. _____		2. _____	
3. _____	4. _____		understood	
5. _____		wrote	6. _____	
take	7. _____		8. _____	
9. _____	10. _____		been	
11. _____		taught	12. _____	
come	13. _____		14. _____	

The present perfect tense is used to tell that you are in the middle of a list of planned activities, the ones that are _already completed_ and the ones that aren't completed _yet_:

I **have worked** three hours.
You **have made** one telephone call.
He **has gone** home.
She **has written** two letters.

We **have eaten** lunch.
You (all) **have ridden** on the train.
They **have bought** their tickets.

The negative forms are a contraction of _have_ or _has_ and _not_:

I **haven't finished** the project.
You **haven't done** your homework.
He **hasn't watched** this movie.
She **hasn't come** in yet.

We **haven't eaten** dinner.
You (all) **haven't ridden** in my new car.
They **haven't paid** the bill.

exercise 13-48

Change the following sentences from the past tense to the present perfect tense.

1. I didn't eat dinner.

_____

2. She didn't leave the station.

_____

3. We didn't look at the menu.

_____

4. He didn't order his lunch.

_____

5. She paid the waiter.

_____

6. We didn't buy anything from a street vendor.

_____

7. I asked for the check.

_____

Verbs Used for Leisure Activities

Review the verbs in the following list. Irregular past tense forms appear after the first slash (/); irregular past participles appear after the second slash:

begin (the game)/began/begun	listen (to music)
catch (the ball)/caught/caught	listen (to the radio)
compete	lose (the game)/lost/lost
dance	participate (in a sport)
go (for a walk)/went/gone	play (a game)
go (to a concert)/went/gone	play (an instrument)
go (to the movies)/went/gone	see (a movie)/saw/seen
go (to the theater)/went/gone	sing/sang/sung
have (a drink with someone)/had/had	start (the game)
have (a party)/had/had	swim/swam/swum
have (coffee with someone)/had/had	throw (the ball)/threw/thrown
have (dinner)/had/had	watch(a game)
have (lunch)/had/had	watch (TV)
hit (the ball)/hit/hit	win the game/won/won
kick (the ball)	

exercise   13-49

Change the sentences from the present tense to the present progressive tense.

1. The game begins. _____

2. He swims. _____

3. They win. _____

4. She throws the ball. _____

5. We sing together. _____

6. I go to the movies. _____

exercise	13-50

Write a yes-or-no question for each of your answers to Exercise 13-49.

1. _____

2. _____

3. _____

4. _____

5. _____

6. _____

exercise	13-51

Make the following sentences negative.

1. He has hit the ball. _____

2. I have seen that movie. _____

3. She has had lunch with him. _____

4. We have sung that song. _____

5. They have danced together before. _____

Asking Questions with *Have*

Questions in the present perfect tense put *have* or *has* between the subject of the sentence and the past participle:

Have I **danced** with you before?   **Have** we **lost** the game?
Have you **seen** the play?   **Have** you (all) **eaten**?
Has he **played** yet?   **Have** they **won** the game?
Has she **gone** for a walk?

exercise	13-52

Write yes-or-no questions for the sentences in Exercise 13-51.

1. _____

2. _____

3. _____

4. _____

5. _____

exercise   13-53

Choose five items from the list of leisure activities and write a sentence for each, telling whether you have or haven't done that activity this month.

1. _____

2. _____

3. _____

4. _____

5. _____

exercise   13-54

Choose five items from the list of leisure activities that you are planning to do, and write a sentence for each in the present progressive tense, telling when you plan to do it.

1. _____

2. _____

3. _____

4. _____

5. _____

Verbs Used for Cooking

Review the verbs in the following list. Irregular past tense forms are indicated after the first slash (/); irregular past participles are indicated after the second slash:

add	grill
arrange	ice (a cake)
bake	marinate
barbecue	microwave
beat/beat/beaten	mix
blend	peel
boil	pour

break (an egg)/broke/broken	process
broil	refrigerate
buy (ingredients)/bought/bought	remove (from oven)
chill	remove (from pan)
chop	sauté
cook	separate (an egg)
cut (into pieces)/cut/cut	simmer
decorate	slice
dice	spread/spread/spread
freeze/froze/frozen	sprinkle
frost (a cake)	stir
fry	strain
garnish	whip

exercise   13-55

*Write the number 1 next to each activity below that involves **preparation before cooking**. Write the number 2 next to each activity that involves **cooking**. Write the number 3 next to each activity that occurs **before serving**.*

1. _____ arrange

2. _____ bake

3. _____ break an egg

4. _____ decorate

5. _____ fry

6. _____ garnish

7. _____ ice a cake

8. _____ marinate

9. _____ mix

10. _____ process

11. _____ sauté

12. _____ simmer

exercise   13-56

Change the following sentences from the present tense to the past tense.

1. I add tomatoes to the sauce.

   _____

2. She ices and decorates the cakes in the morning.

   _____

3. He whips the cream.

   _____

4. They cook for a lot of people.

   _____

5. We grill the fish outside.

   _____

exercise   13-57

Write a yes-or-no question for each of your answers to Exercise 13-56.

1. _____

2. _____

3. _____

4. _____

5. _____

exercise   13-58

Change the following sentences from the past tense to the present perfect tense.

1. We barbecued the chicken.

   _____

2. She removed the pan from the oven.

   _____

3. He arranged the salad on the plates.

_____

4. I peeled the potatoes.

_____

5. They spread butter on the bread.

_____

Giving Directions

The basic verb is used to give commands:

Come here.
Bring me a drink.
Go away.
Turn on the light.

Negative commands are formed by adding *don't* before the verb:

Don't come.
Don't bring me anything.
Don't go.
Don't turn on the light.

exercise 13-59

Circle the verbs that best complete the sentences to form instructions in the kitchen.

1. _____ the tomatoes.

   Ice   **Break**   **Slice**   **Whip**

2. _____ the cake.

   Barbecue   **Ice**   **Fry**   **Strain**

3. _____ the pan from the oven.

   Remove   **Chop**   **Spread**   **Chill**

4. _____ butter on the bread.

   Spread   **Boil**   **Bake**   **Peel**

5. _____ the champagne.

   Dice   **Whip**   **Chill**   **Boil**

6. _____ the eggs into the bowl.

Barbecue   **Freeze**   **Ice**   **Break**

7. _____ a loaf of bread.

Beat   **Boil**   **Bake**   **Peel**

8. _____ water for the tea.

Boil   **Fry**   **Sauté**   **Decorate**

---

exercise   13-60

Change the verbs in Exercise 13-59 to the present progressive tense to write complete sentences that tell what you are in the middle of doing in the kitchen.

1. _____

2. _____

3. _____

4. _____

5. _____

6. _____

7. _____

8. _____

PART IV

ADVERBS

Adverbs are the mechanical tools in our vocabulary. They include words that help us give facts about the states or actions described by verbs. Adverbs enable us to tell where, when, or how often something exists or takes place. For example, "The party is *here*." "The party is *tonight*." "They have a party *every night*." Adverbs enable us to tell in what direction something moves, as in "She is driving *toward* the city." They enable us to tell how an activity is done, for example, "She drives *very carefully*."

Adverbs are important for understanding and giving information about events and activities. Be accurate with adverbs!

Adverbs of Place, Time, and Frequency

Adverbs of Place

Certain adverbs answer the question *Where?* Review the adverbs in the following list:

ahead	in
away	inside
below	nearby
close	nowhere
down	out
downstairs	outside
everywhere	there
far away	up
here	upstairs

exercise   14-1

Match each adverb in the left column with its opposite in the right column.

_____ 1. downstairs   a.   away

_____ 2. here   b.   far away

_____ 3. inside   c.   here

_____ 4. close by/nearby   d.   nowhere

_____ 5. there   e.   outside

_____ 6. everywhere   f.   out

_____ 7. up   g.   upstairs

_____ 8. in   h.   down

An adverb of place after the verb *be* tells the location of a person, place, or thing:

> We are **here**.
> The girls are **inside**.
> Springfield is **nearby**.
> The books are **upstairs**.

exercise   14-2

Write the name of a person, a place, or a thing that is in each of the following locations in relation to where you are now.

1. here _____

2. there _____

3. away _____

4. inside _____

5. outside _____

6. nearby _____

7. far away _____

8. everywhere _____

An adverb of place after a verb of movement indicates where a person or thing goes.

exercise   14-3

Fill in each blank with the adverb described.

1. I want to go (to that place) _____.

2. Please move your car (to where I am) _____.

3. Let's drive (to the other side of town) _____.

4. I'm going (to the interior of the house) _____.

5. She's (not far away) _____.

6. He climbed (to the top of the ladder) _____.

7. He ran (to the floor below) _____.

8. She walked (to where the fresh air is) _____.

Using Prepositional Phrases as Adverbs to Indicate Location

Review the expressions in the following list:

Expressions with *in*	Expressions with *on*	Expressions with *at*
in a building	on a balcony	at a place
in a car	on a bicycle	at a restaurant
in a city	on a bus	at an address
in a corner (inside)	on a corner (outside)	at church
in a house	on a deck	at home
in a private airplane	on a hard chair	at school
in a room	on a horse	at the airport
in a small boat	on a motorcycle	at the beach
in a soft chair	on a patio	at the library
in an office	on a ship	at the office
in bed	on a street	at the zoo
in jail	on a train	at work
in the bathtub	on foot	
in the country	on the floor	
in the garden	on the fourth floor	
in the hospital	on the left side	
in the kitchen	on the metro	
in the middle of a place	on the right side	
in the mountains		
in the water		
in town		

exercise 14-4

Fill in each blank with the most appropriate expression from the previous list.

1. We don't live in the city; we live _____.

2. She visited a farm and rode _____.

3. A friend of mine drives to work _____.

4. He lives _____ of that building.

5. They put the new table _____.

6. She committed a crime, and now she is _____.

7. My cousin had an operation and is still _____.

8. We put the grill and the outdoor furniture _____.

9. My daughter isn't at home now; she's studying _____.

10. I don't drive, so I ride to work _____.

Location and Direction

North	Toronto is in the north of North America.
	Canada is north of the United States.
	We are going north for our summer vacation.
South	Miami is in the south of Florida.
	Florida is south of Georgia.
	The birds fly south in the winter.
East	Washington, D.C., is in the east of the United States.
	Washington, D.C., is east of Virginia.
	The plane is flying east.
West	California is in the west of the United States.
	Texas is west of Louisiana.
	The pioneers moved west.

exercise 14-5

Answer the following questions using words from the list of directions. Use complete sentences.

1. Where do you live?

   _____

2. Where is your home in relation to New York?

   _____

3. Where are you going on your next vacation?

   _____

4. Where is that in relation to where you live?

   _____

5. Where is Mexico?

   _____

Adverbs of Time

Certain adverbs answer the question *When?* Review the adverbs in the following list:

Past	Present	Future
a few days ago	already	afterward
a month ago	no longer	Friday night
a week ago	not yet	later
a year ago	now	next month
before	6:00	next October
last month	still	next Thursday
last night	this afternoon	next week
last Tuesday	this evening	next year
last week	this morning	soon
last year	today	then
recently	tonight	this Friday
ten years ago		tomorrow
then		tomorrow morning
this afternoon		Wednesday afternoon
this morning		
yesterday		

exercise   14-6

Fill in each blank with a word or expression from the previous list.

Assume that today is Sunday, the seventh of August 2005. It is 4:00 P.M.

1. _____ was the sixth of August.

2. _____ is the eighth of August.

3. September is _____.

4. July was _____.

5. The twelfth of August is _____.

6. February 2006 is _____.

7. The seventh of August 1995 was _____.

8. I ate breakfast _____.

9. I will eat dinner _____.

10. My birthday is _____.

Using Prepositional Phrases as Adverbs to Indicate Time

Review the expressions in the following list:

Expressions with *in*	Expressions with *on*	Expressions with *at*
in five years	on holidays	at 5:45 P.M.
in March	on July 15	at midnight
in 1995	on my birthday	at night
in ten minutes	on Tuesday	at noon
in the afternoon	on Tuesdays	at 10:00
in the evening	on weekdays	at 3:30
in the middle of the day	on weekends	at 2:30 A.M.
in the middle of the month		
in the middle of the year		
in the morning		
in 2010		

exercise   14-7

Fill in the blanks with the most appropriate expression from the previous list.

1. It is 3:00. I am leaving in thirty minutes. I am leaving _____.

2. She has classes every Monday through Friday. She has classes _____.

3. I am going on vacation the month after February. I am going on vacation _____.

4. It is 2005. He is going to finish school five years from now. He is going to finish

    _____.

5. We will go to work after we get up tomorrow. We will go to work _____.

Relative Times

before
after
early
late

> My appointment is at 3:00. It is **before** 4:00.
> Tuesday is **before** Wednesday.
> I get off work at 5:00. It is **after** 4:00.
> Thursday is **after** Wednesday.
> Class begins at 6:00 A.M. It is **early** in the morning.
> I get home at 10:00 P.M. It is **late** in the evening.
> Class begins at 9:00. If you come at 8:30, you are **early**.
> If you come at 9:30, you are **late**.

exercise   14-8

Match the expressions in the left column with those in the right column.

_____ 1. 11:30 P.M.   a. after Friday

_____ 2. 5:00 A.M.   b. before Tuesday

_____ 3. after the event has started   c. early

_____ 4. at noon   d. early in the morning

_____ 5. before the event starts   e. early in the year

_____ 6. in January   f. in June

_____ 7. in November   g. in the middle of the day

_____ 8. in the middle of the month   h. late

_____ 9. in the middle of the year   i. late at night

_____ 10. on Monday   j. late in the year

_____ 11. on Saturday   k. on the fifteenth

Adverbs of Frequency

Certain adverbs can answer the question *How often?* Review the adverbs in the following list:

always	often
frequently	rarely
hardly ever	seldom
never	sometimes
occasionally	usually

exercise   14-9

Answer the following questions using adverbs from the previous list. Put the adverb before the verb. Use complete sentences.

1. How often do you ride the metro?

    _____

2. How often does your best friend call you on the telephone?

    _____

3. How often do you sleep eight hours a night?

_____

4. How often do your neighbors have parties?

_____

Certain other expressions indicate how often an activity is performed. These expressions are placed after the verb:

all the time
every day
every so often
once a week
three times a year
twice a month

Answer the following questions using adverbs from the previous list. Use complete sentences.

1. What do you do every so often?

_____

2. How often do you sit down to eat?

_____

3. How often do you go on vacation?

_____

4. What do you do every day?

_____

5. What special occasion happens once a year?

_____

Adverbs of Manner

Certain adverbs indicate how an action is performed.

Forming Adverbs from Adjectives

Many adverbs of manner are formed by adding *-ly* to an adjective:

glad	**gladly**
honest	**honestly**
nice	**nicely**

Adverbs that end in *-y* change the *y* to *i* and then add *-ly*:

easy	**easily**
happy	**happily**
noisy	**noisily**

Adverbs that end in *-ic* add *-ally*:

enthusiastic	**enthusiastically**
tragic	**tragically**

Adverbs that end in *-ble* drop the *e* and add *-y*:

comfortable	**comfortably**
humble	**humbly**

Certain adverbs are the same as the corresponding adjective:

early	**early**
fast	**fast**
hard	**hard**
late	**late**

The adverb for *good* is *well*.

exercise   15-1

Write the adverbs that correspond to the following adjectives.

1. active   _____

2. aggressive   _____

3. bad   _____

4. bitter   _____

5. brave   _____

6. careful   _____

7. cautious   _____

8. charming   _____

9. cheap   _____

10. cheerful   _____

11. civil   _____

12. competent   _____

13. considerate   _____

14. creative   _____

15. efficient   _____

16. faithful   _____

17. fortunate   _____

18. generous   _____

19. glad   _____

20. imaginative   _____

21. interesting   _____

22. kind   _____

23. loud   _____

24. modest   _____

25. natural   _____

26. nervous   _____

27. nice   _____

28. patient   _____

29. pleasant _____

30. polite   _____

31. proper   _____

32. proud   _____

33. quiet   _____

34. reverent _____

35. secure   _____

36. selfish   _____

37. serious   _____

38. sincere   _____

39. skillful _____

40. slow   _____

41. soft   _____

42. successful _____

43. sweet   _____

44. tactful   _____

45. truthful _____

46. weak   _____

exercise   15-2

Write the adverbs that correspond to the following adjectives.

1. capable   _____

2. comfortable   _____

3. easy   _____

4. energetic   _____

5. enthusiastic   _____

6. fast   _____

7. good   _____

8. humble   _____

9. happy   _____

10. noisy   _____

11. reasonable   _____

12. responsible   _____

13. tragic   _____

exercise   15-3

Circle the most appropriate adverb to fill in the blank.

1. He went into the burning house and saved the child. He acted _____.

   tragically   **easily**   **bravely**   **sweetly**

2. She always came to work and completed her assignments on time. She acted _____.

   responsibly   **humbly**   **generously**   **easily**

3. He solved all the math problems right away. He solved them _____.

   easily   **nicely**   **slowly**   **nervously**

4. _____, nobody was injured in the accident.

   Successfully   **Fortunately**   **Proudly**   **Skillfully**

5. That store is great; it always accepts returned items _____.

   selfishly   **actively**   **cheaply**   **cheerfully**

6. The customs agent _____ examined all the packages so as not to do any damage.

   noisily   **carefully**   **aggressively**   **enthusiastically**

7. She _____ accepted the invitation.

   tragically   **truthfully**   **imaginatively**   **gladly**

8. He failed the course because his papers were written very _____.

   badly   **cautiously**   **well**   **capably**

9. She's an artist; everything she does is done _____.

   bitterly   **charmingly**   **creatively**   **quietly**

10. He's a wonderful teacher who answers all your questions very _____.

    aggressively   **actively**   **cheaply**   **patiently**

exercise   15-4

Write a sentence for each of five different people, telling how each one performs a particular activity.

   EXAMPLE: _My friend Jim works quickly._

1. _____

2. _____

3. _____

4. _____

5. _____

Comparing Adverbs

Adverbs of manner can be compared by using _more_ + **adverb** + _than_:

He argues **more** aggressively **than** the other lawyer.
She writes **more** creatively **than** the other students.

exercise   15-5

Write a sentence for each of the following comparisons usng the cues given in parentheses.

1. John drives at fifty-five miles per hour. Mary drives at sixty-five miles per hour. How does John drive? (slowly)

   _____

2. Susan makes only a few mistakes. Janet makes a lot of mistakes. How does Susan work? (carefully)

   _____

3. David makes a lot of noise when he plays. Charles doesn't make noise. How does Charles play? (quietly)

   _____

Certain adverbs have different forms:

badly	**worse than**
early	**earlier than**
fast	**faster than**
hard	**harder than**
late	**later than**
well	**better than**

A negative comparison is made by using *not* + **verb** + *as* + **adverb** + *as*:

> We do**n't** play **as** skillfully **as** the other team.
> She does**n't** play the piano **as** well **as** you.
> He does**n't** run **as** fast **as** his brother.

exercise   15-6

Compare the actions of each of the people you described in Exercise 15-4 with those of another person.

1. _____

2. _____

3. _____

4. _____

5. _____

exercise	15-7

Look at Exercise 15-5 and answer the following questions using a negative comparison.

1. How does Mary drive in comparison with John?

    _____

2. How does Janet work in comparison with Susan?

    _____

3. How does David play in comparison with Charles?

    _____

exercise	15-8

Complete the following chart by writing positive comparisons for the negative examples and negative comparisons for the positive ones.

Positive	Negative
1. more slowly than	_____
2. _____	not as fast as
3. more quietly than	_____
4. _____	not as well as
5. more energetically than	_____
6. _____	not as early as
7. more efficiently than	_____
8. _____	not as patiently as
9. harder than	_____
10. _____	not as seriously as
11. later than	_____
12. _____	not as sweetly as

exercise	15-9

Write five sentences that tell what activities you perform at home or at work and how you do each one.

1. _____

2. _____

3. _____

4. _____

5. _____

exercise	15-10

Compare the way you do the activities you described in Exercise 15-9 with the way someone else does them.

1. _____

2. _____

3. _____

4. _____

5. _____

| Unit 16 | # Adverbs That Modify |

Adverbs That Modify Verbs

Certain adverbs tell how intensely an action is performed:

hardly/scarcely	=	almost not at all
a little/very little	=	some
well enough	=	adequately
really/well	=	very well

The adverbs *hardly, scarcely,* and *really* are placed before the verb they modify:

My car **hardly** runs.

She **scarcely** visits us.

The machine **really** helps.

exercise   16-1

Fill in each blank with the appropriate adverb of intensity.

1. Their new sports car is powerful. It _____ moves.

2. His grandmother is in a wheelchair because she _____ walks.

3. Now that he has studied a year in Mexico, he _____ understands Spanish.

4. Her new boyfriend is so quiet. He _____ said a word at the party.

The adverbs *a little, very little, well enough,* and *well* are placed after the verb they modify:

She sings **a little**.
He plays **well enough**.
They dance **well**.

exercise   16-2

Fill in each blank with the appropriate adverb of intensity.

1. The new employee is not creative, but he's responsible. He works

   _____.

2. She is a great teacher. She is understanding, and she explains the lessons

   _____.

3. I'm not an expert, but I can dance _____.

4. He isn't a great player, but he plays _____.

5. They are excellent speakers. They speak _____.

exercise   16-3

Answer each of the following questions in a complete sentence.

1. What do you hardly do at all?

   _____

2. What do you do a little?

   _____

3. How hard do you work every day?

   _____

4. Who or what really helps you?

   _____

5. What do you do well enough?

   _____

Adverbs That Modify Adjectives and Other Adverbs

Certain adverbs give strength to an adjective:

not at all < fairly < pretty < rather/quite < very < extremely < too

He is **not at all** shy. (He's the opposite of shy.)
He is **fairly** nice. (He's a little bit nice.)
She is **pretty** strict. (She's not a dictator but she maintains discipline.)
We are **rather** tired. (We need a rest before we can do anything else.)
They are **very** expensive. (They cost more than I would like to pay.)
They are **extremely** expensive. (They cost a lot more than I would like to pay.)
They are **too** expensive. (They cost so much that I will not buy them.)

exercise   16-4

Choose the best adverb from the previous list to fill in each blank.

1. When I got home from work I was _____ tired, so I sat down to rest for a while.

2. I'm not going to the party tonight because I am _____ tired.

3. After hiking all day, I was _____ tired.

4. I didn't sleep well last night, so I was _____ tired when I got up.

5. I took a nap when I got home, so I was _____ tired when my guests arrived.

exercise   16-5

Answer each question using adverbs from the previous list to modify the adjectives.

1. What do you do when you are extremely happy?

    _____

2. What do you do if your friends are too busy to go out?

    _____

3. What do your friends do if you are pretty sick?

    _____

4. What does your boss do if you arrive rather late?

    _____

5. What did you think of the last movie you saw?

    _____

6. What is the weather like today?

    _____

7. Are these exercises hard?

    _____

8. What is not at all easy for you?

    _____

A comparison can be made with an adjective by adding the adverb *much* before the comparative form:

>He is **much** taller than I am.
>She is **much** quieter than she was before.
>This movie is **much** better than the other one.
>She's feeling **much** worse.
>She is **much** more aggressive than her sister.

exercise	16-6

Using the cues in parentheses, write sentences that compare the following pairs.

1. Sara is four feet ten inches tall. Her brother is six feet two inches tall. (short)

_____

2. Jackie smiles and talks to everybody. Susan doesn't talk to anybody. (friendly)

_____

3. Joe cleans the house, cooks, and washes the dishes. Jim helps only a little around the house. (helpful)

_____

4. Mary plays volleyball, basketball, softball, soccer, and tennis. Her sister sometimes plays tennis. (athletic)

_____

5. Patricia's baby weighed five pounds. Valerie's baby weighed ten pounds. (small)

_____

The adverbs *fairly, pretty, rather, quite, very, extremely,* and *too* can also modify other adverbs:

>I walk **fairly** fast.
>She reads **pretty** well.
>He works **rather** slowly.
>He drives **very** carefully.
>They work **extremely** hard.
>She speaks **too** softly. (Nobody can hear her.)

exercise   16-7

Use the adverbs from the previous list to answer the following questions about yourself.

1. How well do you cook?

   _____

2. How hard do you work?

   _____

3. What do you do rather quickly?

   _____

4. Do you sleep well?

   _____

5. What do you do too slowly?

   _____

exercise   16-8

Use the adverbs from the previous list to answer the following questions about someone you know.

1. How well does he or she cook?

   _____

2. How hard does he or she work?

   _____

3. What does he or she do rather quickly?

   _____

4. Does he or she drive well?

   _____

5. How hard does he or she work?

   _____

Answer Key

Part I Nouns
Unit 1 People and Places

1-1
1. grandmother
2. grandfather
3. aunt
4. uncle
5. cousin
6. son-in-law
7. Answers will vary.
8. Answers will vary.

1-2
1. f
2. g
3. i.
4. d
5. h
6. e
7. a
8. c
9. b

1-3
1. doctor
2. police officer
3. neighbor
4. pharmacist
5. dentist

1-4
1. cheeks . . . chin . . . ears . . . eyes . . . face . . . hair . . . lips . . . mouth . . . nose
2. arm
3. knee
4. wrist
5. ankle
6. toes . . . fingers . . . thumb
7. neck . . . arm
8. waist

1-5
1. road
2. library
3. sun
4. farm
5. apartment
6. moon
7. post office
8. highway

1-6
Answers will vary.

1-7
Answers will vary.

1-8
Answers will vary.

1-9
Answers will vary.

1-10

1. bathroom
2. bedroom
3. bedroom
4. classroom
5. bedroom
6. any room
7. any room
8. dining room
9. classroom, office
10. any room
11. bathroom, bedroom, hall, kitchen
12. kitchen
13. living room
14. library, office
15. library, office
16. kitchen, restaurant, store
17. dining room, kitchen, restaurant, any room
18. classroom, office
19. kitchen, laundry room
20. dining room, kitchen, restaurant
21. kitchen, restaurant
22. bedroom
23. laundry room
24. department store
25. department store
26. bathroom
27. office
28. office
29. living room
30. dining room, kitchen, restaurant
31. kitchen, restaurant
32. dining room, kitchen, restaurant, any room
33. dining room, kitchen, restaurant
34. any room
35. any room
36. kitchen, restaurant
37. dining room, kitchen, restaurant
38. any room
39. bedroom
40. classroom, office, any room
41. kitchen, restaurant
42. classroom, office, any room
43. classroom, office, any room
44. classroom, office, any room
45. bedroom, living room
46. bedroom
47. kitchen, dining room, restaurant
48. classroom, library, office
49. kitchen, restaurant
50. kitchen, dining room, restaurant
51. bedroom
52. bathroom
53. bathroom, kitchen, laundry room, restaurant
54. bathroom, kitchen, laundry room
55. living room
56. dining room, kitchen, restaurant
57. hall
58. kitchen, restaurant
59. any room
60. kitchen
61. any room
62. kitchen, restaurant
63. bathroom
64. bathroom, kitchen
65. bedroom, living room, any room
66. laundry room

Unit 2 Singular, Plural, and Noncount Nouns

2-1

1. a
2. an
3. an
4. an
5. a
6. a
7. a
8. an
9. a
10. a
11. a
12. an
13. a
14. a
15. an
16. an
17. an
18. a
19. an
20. an
21. a
22. a
23. a
24. an
25. a
26. an
27. an
28. a
29. a
30. a
31. an
32. an
33. an
34. a
35. an
36. a
37. a
38. an
39. an
40. an

2-2

1. I have a book.
2. There is an answer key.
3. There is a *t*.
4. There is one *e*.

2-3

1. a class
2. a band . . . an orchestra
3. a company
4. a family
5. a team
6. a government
7. a committee
8. a choir . . . a chorus

2-4

1. brothers
2. daughters
3. wives
4. babies
5. children
6. men
7. women
8. teenagers
9. artists
10. customers
11. students
12. actresses
13. bosses
14. nurses
15. eyes
16. ears
17. toes
18. churches
19. cities
20. libraries
21. bus stops
22. post offices
23. windows
24. glasses
25. knives
26. forks
27. stoves
28. facecloths

2-5

1. bands
2. choirs
3. choruses
4. classes
5. committees
6. families
7. governments
8. orchestras
9. teams

2-6   Answers will vary.

2-7   Answers will vary.

2-8   Answers will vary.

2-9

1. an OR one . . . a OR one
2. an OR one . . . an OR one
3. some OR a lot of OR a few OR any . . . some OR a lot of OR a few OR any OR two
4. a OR one . . . some OR a few OR a lot of
5. a OR one
6. some OR two OR a few
7. any
8. some OR a lot of OR a few OR two
9. some OR a few OR two
10. a . . . some OR two

2-10   Answers will vary.

2-11   Answers will vary.

2-12   Answers will vary.

2-13   Answers will vary.

2-14

1. a little, a lot of, some, no, a slice of
2. three slices of
3. a little, some, three bowls of, a gallon of, two quarts of
4. a glass of, three glasses of, some, a little
5. some, a little, two bags of
6. a piece of, two pieces of, a little, some
7. some, a piece of, two pieces of, a lot of
8. some, a piece of, no
9. two, a few, some, no
10. a glass of, two glasses of, some, a lot of

2-15   Answers will vary.

2-16
1. a little
2. no, some, a little
3. some, a lot of
4. some, a little
5. too much, a lot of

2-17   Answers will vary.

2-18
1. an
2. Ø
3. Ø
4. Ø . . . Ø
5. Ø
6. a . . . Ø . . . a
7. Ø
8. Ø
9. Ø
10. a . . . a

2-19
1. a
2. the
3. Ø
4. the
5. Ø
6. the
7. the
8. the
9. Ø
10. the

2-20   Answers will vary.

2-21   Answers will vary.

2-22   Answers will vary.

2-23
1. a
2. Ø
3. The
4. Ø
5. the

2-24
1. This
2. those
3. that
4. these
5. that
6. those
7. these
8. this

Unit 3 Proper Nouns

3-1
1. She's reading a book called *A Guide to Good Manners.*
2. We have to go to the **S**pringfield **L**ibrary on **M**onday.
3. They are from **I**taly, and they don't speak **S**panish.
4. **D**avid is going to go to **W**ilson **A**cademy for **B**oys in **S**eptember.

3-2   Answers will vary.

Unit 4 Possessive Nouns and Pronouns

4-1

1. my sister's car
2. the men's hats
3. the children's party
4. the doctor's office
5. the girls' apartment
6. Miss Smith's class
7. Ben Lindsay's school
8. the ladies' meeting

4-2

Answers will vary.

4-3

1. her car
2. their hats
3. their party
4. his/her office
5. their apartment
6. her class
7. his school
8. their meeting

4-4

Answers will vary.

Unit 5 Review of Singular, Plural, and Noncount Nouns

5-1

1. too many
2. an
3. the
4. Those
5. a little
6. a lot of
7. too much
8. no
9. John's
10. some

5-2

1. one bottle/four bottles
2. these letters/that information
3. a few pills/a little medicine
4. too much sugar/one spoonful/a few spoonfuls
5. too many chairs/not much furniture/a chair
6. a necklace/these earrings/a little jewelry
7. that fruit/those vegetables
8. There is a nail/There are screws/There is hardware
9. There is one lamp/There are no lights/There is no water
10. Here is your letter/There are no letters

Unit 6 Verbs Used as Nouns

6-1

1. waiting
2. Driving
3. living
4. cooking
5. Studying
6. staying

6-2

Answers will vary.

Unit 7 More Specific Nouns

7-1
1. boys OR girls OR kids
2. dude OR guy OR youth
3. young lady
4. bum

7-2
1. fiancé
2. roommate
3. coworkers OR colleagues
4. acquaintance

7-3
1. e
2. c OR g
3. b OR c OR g
4. c OR g OR h
5. d
6. c OR f OR g
7. g
8. b OR c OR g
9. a
10. a OR i

7-4   Answers will vary.

7-5   Answers will vary.

7-6   Answers will vary.

7-7   Answers will vary.

7-8
1. d
2. f
3. e
4. b
5. a
6. c

7-9   Answers will vary.

7-10
1. g
2. b
3. h
4. f
5. d
6. j
7. e
8. a
9. c

7-11
1. e
2. f
3. b
4. h
5. a
6. d
7. g
8. c

7-12   Answers will vary.

7-13   Answers will vary.

7-14   Answers will vary.

7-15 Answers will vary.

7-16 Answers will vary.

7-17
1. c
2. d
3. a
4. e
5. f
6. b

7-18
1. hurricane
2. gale
3. sandstorm
4. tornado

Part II Adjectives
Unit 8 Making Descriptions

8-1 Answers will vary.

8-2
1. handicapped
2. shy
3. little
4. cowardly
5. ugly
6. slow
7. thin
8. unfriendly
9. stingy

8-3
1. bad
2. boring
3. small
4. energetic
5. kind
6. young
7. plain
8. humble
9. noisy

8-4
1. poor
2. serious
3. dumb
4. easygoing
5. bitter
6. short
7. happy
8. strong

8-5
1. incapable
2. incompetent
3. inconsiderate
4. inefficient
5. insecure
6. insincere
7. intolerant
8. immodest
9. impatient
10. impolite
11. improper
12. irresistible
13. irreverent
14. unbalanced
15. uncivil
16. uncivilized
17. undisciplined
18. unenthusiastic
19. unfaithful
20. unfortunate
21. unhappy
22. unhealthy
23. unkind
24. unnatural
25. unpleasant
26. unpopular
27. unreasonable
28. unselfish
29. unsuccessful
30. untidy
31. untrustworthy
32. untruthful

8-6
1. careless
2. unfaithful
3. harmless
4. unsuccessful
5. tactless
6. untruthful

8-7

1. intelligent	10. flexible	19. friendly
2. persistent	11. optimistic	20. lonely
3. independent	12. pessimistic	21. imaginative
4. insistent	13. athletic	22. manipulative
5. hospitable	14. materialistic	23. persuasive
6. likable	15. idealistic	24. aggressive
7. responsible	16. lovely	25. appreciative
8. adorable	17. lively	
9. gullible	18. cowardly	

8-8

1. a
2. an
3. an
4. a
5. an

8-9

Answers will vary.

8-10

Answers will vary.

8-11

1. hungry
2. busy
3. ready
4. thirsty
5. upset
6. cold

8-12

1. anxious/upset/nervous
2. hot
3. alive
4. clean
5. sad/depressed
6. full
7. dissatisfied
8. well
9. rested
10. cool

8-13

Answers will vary.

8-14

1. narrow
2. big/large
3. light
4. tiny
5. short

8-15

Answers will vary.

8-16

Answers will vary.

8-17

Answers will vary.

8-18

1. h
2. a
3. i
4. b
5. c
6. d
7. g
8. j
9. l
10. e
11. k
12. f

8-19

1. empty
2. new
3. patched
4. messy
5. dirty
6. broken
7. fresh

8-20   Answers will vary.

 8-21
1. expensive
2. spacious
3. empty
4. dry
5. safe
6. light
7. unfurnished
8. well-maintained
9. open
10. old-fashioned

 8-22   Answers will vary.

 8-23
Pleasant: breezy, clear, cool, dry, nice, pleasant, sunny, warm
Unpleasant: chilly, cloudy, cold, foggy, freezing, hot, humid, icy, rainy, stormy, unpleasant, windy

8-24
1. freezing (Answers may vary.)
2. cold OR freezing OR icy OR unpleasant
3. pleasant (Answers may vary.)
4. Answers will vary.
5. hot (Answers may vary.)
6. foggy OR icy OR rainy OR stormy
7. rainy
8. cold OR freezing OR sunny
9. breezy OR windy
10. chilly

Unit 9 Comparisons and Superlatives

9-1
1. pretty
2. not at all
3. very
4. very
5. pretty

9-2   Answers will vary.

 9-3
These are possible answers, but all may vary.
1. I didn't eat it.
2. We stayed home.
3. I got sick.
4. She got a ticket.
5. I'm not going to buy them.

9-4   Answers will vary.

9-5
1. brighter
2. cheaper
3. cleaner
4. colder
5. cooler
6. damper
7. darker
8. faster
9. fresher
10. higher
11. lighter
12. longer
13. neater
14. newer
15. older
16. plainer
17. poorer
18. richer
19. shorter
20. sicker
21. slower
22. smaller
23. smarter
24. sweeter
25. taller
26. younger

 9-6
1. cuter
2. finer
3. lamer
4. looser
5. nicer
6. paler
7. ruder
8. tamer
9. wider

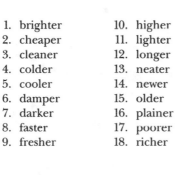

9-7

1. bigger
2. fatter
3. fitter
4. hotter
5. madder
6. redder
7. sadder
8. thinner

9-8

Answers will vary.

9-9

1. angrier
2. bossier
3. busier
4. cloudier
5. cozier
6. crazier
7. dirtier
8. easier
9. friendlier
10. funnier
11. happier
12. lazier
13. lonelier
14. lovelier
15. luckier
16. noisier
17. prettier
18. rainier
19. sillier
20. sunnier
21. tastier
22. uglier

9-10

1. quieter
2. simpler
3. narrower
4. gentler
5. crueler
6. littler

9-11

1. more athletic
2. more boring
3. more civil
4. more civilized
5. cleaner
6. more comfortable
7. more considerate
8. cooler
9. more delicious
10. dirtier
11. fresher
12. friendlier
13. gentler
14. more gullible
15. healthier
16. hotter
17. more open
18. more patient
19. more persuasive
20. more pleasant
21. more proper
22. prouder
23. quieter
24. ruder
25. sadder
26. more serious
27. sicker
28. sillier
29. more sincere
30. slower
31. smaller
32. stingier
33. more successful
34. sweeter
35. tinier
36. more unfriendly
37. more upset
38. more useful
39. wider
40. more worried

9-12

1. prettier than
2. not as comfortable as
3. not as good as
4. better than
5. not as big as

9-13

1. worst
2. cleanest
3. coldest
4. craziest
5. cutest
6. friendliest
7. gentlest
8. best
9. hottest
10. silliest
11. luckiest
12. maddest
13. neatest
14. nicest
15. rudest
16. saddest

9-14

Answers will vary.

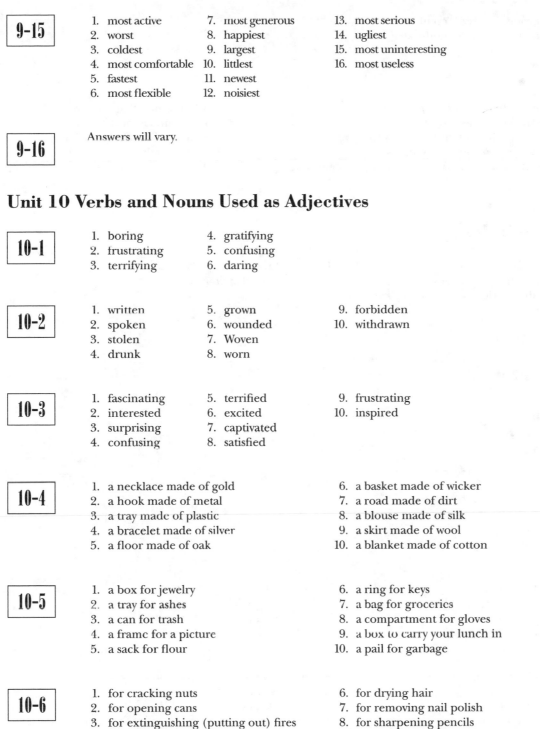

9-15

1. most active
2. worst
3. coldest
4. most comfortable
5. fastest
6. most flexible
7. most generous
8. happiest
9. largest
10. littlest
11. newest
12. noisiest
13. most serious
14. ugliest
15. most uninteresting
16. most useless

9-16   Answers will vary.

Unit 10 Verbs and Nouns Used as Adjectives

10-1

1. boring
2. frustrating
3. terrifying
4. gratifying
5. confusing
6. daring

10-2

1. written
2. spoken
3. stolen
4. drunk
5. grown
6. wounded
7. Woven
8. worn
9. forbidden
10. withdrawn

10-3

1. fascinating
2. interested
3. surprising
4. confusing
5. terrified
6. excited
7. captivated
8. satisfied
9. frustrating
10. inspired

10-4

1. a necklace made of gold
2. a hook made of metal
3. a tray made of plastic
4. a bracelet made of silver
5. a floor made of oak
6. a basket made of wicker
7. a road made of dirt
8. a blouse made of silk
9. a skirt made of wool
10. a blanket made of cotton

10-5

1. a box for jewelry
2. a tray for ashes
3. a can for trash
4. a frame for a picture
5. a sack for flour
6. a ring for keys
7. a bag for groceries
8. a compartment for gloves
9. a box to carry your lunch in
10. a pail for garbage

10-6

1. for cracking nuts
2. for opening cans
3. for extinguishing (putting out) fires
4. for playing CDs
5. for breaking up ice
6. for drying hair
7. for removing nail polish
8. for sharpening pencils
9. for removing spots
10. for polishing floors

10-7   Answers will vary.

10-8

1. a bicycle lock
2. a mailbox key
3. a rose garden
4. homework
5. a student desk

1. hardheaded
2. sure-footed
3. single-minded
4. long-winded

5. evenhanded
6. hotheaded

1. a plan for the next five years
2. a warranty that lasts three years
3. a guarantee that lasts as long as you are living
4. a discussion that lasts ten minutes
5. a weight (or dumbbell) that weighs three pounds

6. a vacation that lasts two weeks
7. a contract for two years
8. a meeting that lasts all day
9. a party that lasts all night
10. something that happens every day

Unit 11 Adjective Order

1. a long black silk skirt
2. new Italian leather shoes
3. beautiful Mexican silver earrings

4. a rich three-layer birthday cake
5. a heavy round antique mirror

Answers will vary.

Part III Verbs
Unit 12 The Verb *Be*

12-1

1. is
2. are
3. is

4. are
5. are
6. am

12-2

Answers will vary.

12-3

1. Is he here now?
2. Are you happy?
3. Am I sitting down?
4. Is he asking directions?

5. Are they building a new house?
6. Is she turning left?
7. Is he taking photographs?
8. Is she riding a bicycle?

12-4

1. He isn't here now.
2. You're not happy.
3. I'm not sitting down.
4. He isn't asking directions.

5. They aren't building a new house.
6. She isn't turning left.
7. He isn't taking photographs.
8. She isn't riding a bicycle.

12-5

1. was
2. were
3. was

4. were
5. were
6. was

12-6 Answers will vary but should include these verbs.

1. I was . . .
2. . . . was with me.
3. I was . . . OR We were . . .
4. It was . . .
5. No, nobody else was there. OR Yes, ____ was there. OR Yes, ____ and ____ were there.

Unit 13 Non–*To Be* Verbs

13-1
1. h	5. f	9. d
2. i	6. g	10. c
3. e	7. a	
4. j	8. b	

13-2
1. sounds	4. smell
2. appear	5. seems
3. feel	6. resembles

13-3
1. matches	5. goes	9. does
2. eats	6. wishes	10. dances
3. has	7. cleans	
4. drinks	8. dries	

13-4
1. cleaned	4. walked
2. opened	5. watched
3. worked	

13-5
1. stopped	4. exercised
2. closed	5. tried
3. shopped	

13-6
1. listened	5. cried	9. planned
2. laughed	6. exercised	10. watched
3. turned	7. brushed	
4. dreamed	8. smiled	

13-7 Answers will vary.

13-8 Answers will vary.

13-9 Answers will vary.

13-10
1. makes	4. vacuum
2. water	5. pays
3. clean	

13-11

Answers will vary.

13-12

Answers will vary.

13-13

1. sweep the floor
2. do the shopping
3. iron clothes
4. make appointments
5. wash the windows OR clean up the mess
6. pay bills
7. make repairs
8. clean up the yard OR mow the lawn OR take out the trash OR water plants OR weed the garden
9. do laundry
10. dust the furniture

13-14

Answers will vary.

13-15

1. answered	6. learned	11. spelled
2. asked	7. listened	12. studied
3. corrected	8. paid	13. used
4. erased	9. played	
5. helped	10. solved	

13-16

1. taught	5. made	9. read
2. wrote	6. did	10. paid
3. understood	7. drew	
4. took	8. took	

13-17

1. He doesn't get up at 6:00.
2. They don't eat breakfast together every morning.
3. She doesn't dream during the day.
4. We don't buy groceries every week.
5. I don't laugh a lot.

13-18

1. My mother didn't teach me to read and write.
2. He didn't write her an e-mail last week.
3. I didn't understand today's lesson.
4. We didn't take a hard test this morning.
5. You didn't make only one mistake.
6. They didn't do all of the exercises.
7. They didn't draw pictures in class.
8. My friend and I didn't take turns with the computer.
9. She didn't read us a wonderful story.
10. I hope you didn't pay attention.

13-19

Answers will vary.

13-20

Answers will vary.

13-21
1. Do you write e-mail?
2. Does he search the Internet?
3. Does she use the computer?
4. Do you all attend meetings?
5. Do they answer the telephone?
6. Do we take coffee breaks?

13-22
1. What goes in that file?
2. Who answers the telephone?
3. When do you search the Internet?
4. Where do we send faxes?
5. Where do they write the reports?

13-23
1. Did they take a long coffee break?
2. Did she answer the telephone?
3. Did Mary write these e-mails?
4. Did you search the Internet this afternoon?
5. Did John organize all your files?

13-24
1. Who wrote a letter today?
2. What did he do yesterday?
3. When did John call you?
4. Where did you eat on Monday night?
5. How did she go home?

13-25
Answers will vary.

13-26
Answers will vary.

13-27
Answers will vary.

13-28
Answers will vary.

13-29
1. Do you return clothes that don't fit?
2. Does she always use her credit card?
3. Does she like her new shoes?
4. Do you want these shirts?
5. Does he like to go shopping?

13-30
1. Did she buy a new dress?
2. Did he forget to give you a receipt?
3. Did you try on a lot of clothes?
4. Did she go shopping yesterday?
5. Did you buy anything?

13-31
1. Who always gets a bargain?
2. What did you do for thirty minutes?
3. Where did they spend a lot of money?
4. Who does he always thank?
5. When did you write the check?
6. How much did it cost?

13-32
1. lost my checkbook
2. drove up to the drive-up window
3. make a deposit
4. withdraw cash
5. buy a CD

13-33
1. They didn't close their account.
2. This account doesn't earn interest.
3. I didn't get a new PIN.
4. He didn't withdraw cash.
5. She doesn't make a deposit every week.

13-34
1. Did you pay an installment last month?
2. Did you want to open an account?
3. When did she buy a CD?
4. What did he do?
5. Who withdrew cash?

13-35   Answers will vary.

13-36
1. He is cashing a check.
2. I am withdrawing money.
3. They are opening an account.
4. We are applying for a loan.
5. The investment is earning interest.
6. She is getting cash from the ATM.
7. I am saving money.
8. He is paying an installment on his loan.

13-37   Answers will vary.

13-38   Answers will vary.

13-39
1. Where did you have a picnic?
2. Who gets off the bus here?
3. Did he take a lot of photographs?
4. Did she lie in the sun for an hour?
5. What does he always buy?

13-40
1. She doesn't ask directions.
2. We don't turn left here.
3. He doesn't drive a car.
4. They don't get lost.
5. I don't go jogging.

13-41
1. We didn't see an accident.
2. They didn't have a picnic.
3. He didn't get on the bus.
4. You didn't turn right.
5. She didn't get out of the car.

13-42
1. was, were
2. became
3. built
4. bought
5. came
6. did
7. drew
8. drank
9. drove
10. ate
11. felt
12. found
13. got
14. went
15. grew
16. had
17. heard
18. lay
19. made
20. paid
21. put
22. left
23. read
24. rode
25. ran
26. saw
27. sat
28. slept
29. spent
30. stood
31. swept
32. took
33. taught
34. thought
35. understood
36. woke up
37. withdrew
38. wrote

13-43
1. He is getting off the elevator.
2. We are ordering our meal.
3. She is paying the waiter.
4. We are leaving the station.
5. They are going through the revolving doors.

13-44
1. He isn't leaving the building.
2. She isn't enjoying her meal.
3. They aren't riding on the escalator.
4. I'm not looking at the menu.
5. He's not talking on his cell phone.

13-45
1. Is he leaving the building?
2. Is she enjoying her meal?
3. Are they riding on the escalator?
4. Are you looking at the menu?
5. Is he talking on his cell phone?

13-46
1. She hasn't asked directions.
2. We haven't turned left here.
3. He hasn't driven a car.
4. They haven't gotten lost.
5. I haven't gone jogging.

13-47
1. ate
2. eaten
3. understand
4. understood
5. write
6. written
7. took
8. taken
9. be
10. was, were
11. teach
12. taught
13. came
14. come

13-48
1. I haven't eaten dinner.
2. She hasn't left the station.
3. We haven't looked at the menu.
4. He hasn't ordered his lunch.
5. She has paid the waiter.
6. We haven't bought anything from a street vendor.
7. I have asked for the check.

13-49
1. The game is beginning.
2. He is swimming.
3. They are winning.
4. She is throwing the ball.
5. We are singing together.
6. I am going to the movies.

13-50
1. Is the game beginning?
2. Is he swimming?
3. Are they winning?
4. Is she throwing the ball?
5. Are you singing together?
6. Are you going to the movies?

13-51
1. He hasn't hit the ball.
2. I haven't seen that movie.
3. She hasn't had lunch with him.
4. We haven't sung that song.
5. They haven't danced together before.

13-52
1. Has he hit the ball?
2. Have you seen that movie?
3. Has she had lunch with him?
4. Have you/we sung that song?
5. Have they danced together before?

13-53
Answers will vary.

13-54
Answers will vary.

13-55
1. 3
2. 2
3. 1
4. 3
5. 2
6. 3
7. 3
8. 1
9. 1
10. 1
11. 2
12. 2

13-56
1. I added tomatoes to the sauce.
2. She iced and decorated the cakes in the morning.
3. He whipped the cream.
4. They cooked for a lot of people.
5. We grilled the fish outside.

13-57
1. Did you add tomatoes to the sauce?
2. Did she ice and decorate the cakes in the morning?
3. Did he whip the cream?
4. Did they cook for a lot of people?
5. Did you grill the fish outside?

13-58
1. We have barbecued the chicken.
2. She has removed the pan from the oven.
3. He has arranged the salad on the plates.
4. I have peeled the potatoes.
5. They have spread butter on the bread.

13-59
1. Slice
2. Ice
3. Remove
4. Spread
5. Chill
6. Break
7. Bake
8. Boil

13-60
1. I am slicing the tomatoes.
2. I am icing the cake.
3. I am removing the pan from the oven.
4. I am spreading butter on the bread.
5. I am chilling the champagne.
6. I am breaking the eggs into the bowl.
7. I am baking a loaf of bread.
8. I am boiling water for the tea.

Part IV Adverbs
Unit 14 Adverbs of Place, Time, and Frequency

14-1
1. g
2. a
3. e
4. b
5. c
6. d
7. h
8. f

14-2   Answers will vary.

14-3
1. there
2. here
3. there
4. inside
5. nearby
6. up
7. downstairs
8. outside

14-4
1. in the country
2. on a horse
3. in a car
4. on the fourth floor
5. in the kitchen
6. in jail
7. in the hospital
8. on a balcony OR on a deck OR on a patio
9. at school OR at the library
10. on a bicycle OR on a bus OR on a train OR on the metro

14-5   Answers will vary.

14-6
1. Yesterday
2. Tomorrow
3. next month
4. last month
5. this Friday
6. next year
7. ten years ago
8. this morning
9. this evening OR tonight
10. Answers will vary.

14-7
1. at 3:30
2. on weekdays
3. in March
4. in 2010
5. in the morning

14-8
1. i
2. d
3. h
4. g
5. c
6. e
7. j
8. k
9. f
10. b
11. a

14-9 Answers will vary.

14-10 Answers will vary.

Unit 15 Adverbs of Manner

15-1

1. actively
2. aggressively
3. badly
4. bitterly
5. bravely
6. carefully
7. cautiously
8. charmingly
9. cheaply
10. cheerfully
11. civilly
12. competently
13. considerately
14. creatively
15. efficiently
16. faithfully
17. fortunately
18. generously
19. gladly
20. imaginatively
21. interestingly
22. kindly
23. loudly
24. modestly
25. naturally
26. nervously
27. nicely
28. patiently
29. pleasantly
30. politely
31. properly
32. proudly
33. quietly
34. reverently
35. securely
36. selfishly
37. seriously
38. sincerely
39. skillfully
40. slowly
41. softly
42. successfully
43. sweetly
44. tactfully
45. truthfully
46. weakly

15-2

1. capably
2. comfortably
3. easily
4. energetically
5. enthusiastically
6. fast
7. well
8. humbly
9. happily
10. noisily
11. reasonably
12. responsibly
13. tragically

15-3

1. bravely
2. responsibly
3. easily
4. Fortunately
5. cheerfully
6. carefully
7. gladly
8. badly
9. creatively
10. patiently

15-4 Answers will vary.

15-5
1. John drives more slowly than Mary.
2. Susan works more carefully than Janet.
3. Charles plays more quietly than David.

15-6 Answers will vary.

15-7
1. Mary doesn't drive as slowly as John.
2. Janet doesn't work as carefully as Susan.
3. David doesn't play as quietly as Charles.

15-8

1. not as slowly as
2. faster than
3. not as quietly as
4. better than
5. not as energetically as
6. earlier than
7. not as efficiently as
8. more patiently than
9. not as hard as
10. more seriously than
11. not as late as
12. more sweetly than

15-9   Answers will vary.

15-10   Answers will vary.

Unit 16 Adverbs That Modify

16-1
1. really
2. hardly OR scarcely
3. really
4. hardly OR scarcely

16-2
1. well enough
2. well
3. a little OR well enough
4. a little OR well enough
5. well

16-3   Answers will vary.

16-4
1. pretty OR rather OR quite OR very
2. too OR extremely OR very
3. extremely OR very
4. pretty OR rather OR quite
5. not at all

16-5   Answers will vary.

16-6
1. Sara is much shorter than her brother.
2. Jackie is much friendlier than Susan.
3. Joe is much more helpful than Jim.
4. Mary is much more athletic than her sister.
5. Patricia's baby was much smaller than Valerie's.

16-7   Answers will vary.

16-8   Answers will vary.

necessary, continue repeating steps 3 and 4 until one of the thermometers reaches the target temperature.

Questions and Conclusions

1. What happened to the temperatures when the light was turned on?

2. How difficult was it to find the position on the meter stick where the final temperature matched the target temperature? Why was this so?

3. How does distance from a source of light (the Sun, for example) affect temperature?

4. How would the temperatures on the gaseous planets (all the planets beyond Mars except Pluto) compare to the temperatures on Mercury, Venus, Earth, and Mars (the terrestrial planets)?

5. What are some other factors besides distance from the Sun that determine the average temperature of the planet?

6. Based on your observations, do you think we could still live on Earth if the planet moved very much toward or away from the Sun? Why?

7. If Mars or Venus were somehow moved so they were now the same distance from the Sun as Earth, do you think we could live on either of them? Why or why not?

The Goldilocks Effect or "This Planet Is Just Right!"

Materials

For each group of students:

◊ 4 Celsius thermometers

◊ meter stick

◊ reflector lamp (equipped with clamp) or gooseneck lamp with 75-watt bulb

◊ watch or clock

Vocabulary

Clement zone: A narrow range of distances from the Sun in which conditions are suitable to sustain life as we know it.

What Is Happening?

The fact that Earth is the only planet in the Solar System that we know supports life is a consequence primarily of its distance from the Sun. If Earth were only *two* percent of its present distance farther away from the Sun, it would be like Mars; a permanent "Ice Age" wasteland with a carbon dioxide atmosphere and all of its water tied up in polar ice caps. If Earth were only *five* percent closer to the Sun, it would be most like Venus, a planet many astronomers have described as a "hellish place." The surface temperature on Venus is about 454° C. Earth's distance from the Sun is just right, and practically no other distance will do. Only recently has it been determined that the range of distances from the Sun in which Earth's conditions could have formed is very small compared to the scale of the Solar System. Because of this narrow range (or **clement zone**), Earth's atmosphere is the only one in the Solar System which will allow water to exist in all three states simultaneously—solid, liquid, and gas.

Earth's distance from the Sun has allowed life to flourish here because of one of the properties of light: As the distance from a light source increases, the intensity of the light decreases. That is why in a room with only one light, it becomes increasingly difficult to read a book as you move farther away from the source. The intensity of the light decreases with the *square* of the distance from the source. This means that if you move twice as far away from the source, the intensity of the light will be only one-fourth of what it was. Earth is placed such that it gets just the right intensity of light to allow its unique atmosphere to exist.

This activity is designed to show students that distance from a light source will affect temperature and that the range of distances in which a specific temperature can exist is relatively small.

Important Points for Students to Understand

◊ The intensity of light decreases as you move away from the source.

◊ As the intensity of light decreases, the temperature resulting from that light will also decrease.

◊ The temperature on a planet is primarily a consequence of the planet's distance from the Sun. But there are other factors as well.

◊ The range of distances from the Sun in which life can exist is very narrow.

Time Management

Including set up and clean up, this activity will take one class period or less. It is suggested that students have another task to do between temperature readings. For example, they could be completing an assignment on planetary comparisons which emphasizes the uniqueness of Earth.

Preparation

Prior to the class, assemble all the materials in a central location. Make sure that all lamps are working and that none of the thermometers are broken.

Prior to the class period, set up an apparatus and place one thermometer someplace on the meter stick. Turn the light on and allow it to remain on until the temperature on the thermometer no longer rises. Let this temperature be the "target temperature" mentioned in the student instructions. Students will try to determine where on the meter stick to place a thermometer so that its temperature matches the target temperature.

Be sure that thermometers are calibrated. Also, be sure that room temperature does not change much between the time the target temperature is determined and the time the activity is done. If the room temperature changes too much, the target temperature may actually be below room temperature, making the activity impossible. For additional information, refer to Reading 7, Reading 9, "Grand Theme 2: Atmosphere, Oceans, Cryosphere, and Hydrologic Cycle;" and Reading 8, "After the Warming."

Suggestions for Further Study

Some students may want to further investigate the relationship between intensity and distance from a light source. This can be done easily in a room with a single light source and a light meter. This provides an excellent opportunity to use graphing skills, plotting distance versus light intensity.

There are other factors which determine a planet's surface temperature besides light intensity, in particular the atmosphere. The atmosphere affects temperature through a phenomenon known as the greenhouse effect. In addition to extensive literature on this topic, there are activities which demonstrate it quite well, such as Activity 8, "The Greenhouse Effect."

Suggestions for Interdisciplinary Reading and Study

The book *This Island Earth* provides an interesting perspective of Earth. It describes the planet as one of the nine in the Solar System, emphasizing its beauty and uniqueness among the others. Earth is "just right" in many different ways. Some of the passages from this book have been included in the Readings. The "Quotes from Space," appearing at the beginning of Activities 8 and 9, are quotes from astronauts from shuttle and Apollo missions describing what Earth looks like from space. Their accounts provide us with a unique perspective on our planet. The descriptions highlight Earth's beautiful and fragile nature. Encourage students to read these accounts and react to them in small group or class discussions. What do these descriptions make the students realize about Earth that they did not realize before?

The beauty and fragility of Earth are becoming more and more apparent through NASA's "Mission to Planet Earth." The purpose of the mission is to study Earth in the same way all the other planets have been studied—from the outside looking in. This is being accomplished by satellites orbiting Earth. Some of the background literature on the mission stresses the "just right-ness" of Earth (see Readings 7, 9, and 11). Encourage students to find out more about the Mission to Planet Earth and its discoveries.

Answers to Questions for Students

1. All the temperatures rise, but those closer to the light source rise by a greater amount and more rapidly.

2. Answers will depend on the students. It may be difficult to find the position since the range of distances from the light source which accompany the target temperature is small.

3. As distance increases, radiant energy decreases.

4. Since they are farther away, they should be lower than the temperatures of the inner planets.

5. The atmosphere. The amount of liquid water. For example, Earth's atmosphere helps keep a lot of heat in, and the ocean currents moderate temperatures all over the planet.

6. No. Because a very small change in the distance from the Sun leads to very drastic changes in conditions on Earth, most notably in temperature.

7. Answers will vary. There is quite a bit of evidence that neither planet would be habitable even if it were in the position of Earth. Evidence from the geologic record suggests that Earth took billions of years to evolve life-sustaining conditions.

Quote from Space

. . . One view in particular is awe-inspiring with Africa in the foreground and the whole profile of the Mediterranean very clear. One stares at the whole Mediterranean, looking from outer space much as in an atlas, but not as in a drawing. Much of our most commonly taught history centers around that little sea, a mere patch of the hemisphere, which once seemed to its inhabitants to be the whole world.

Looking into the blackness beyond the sharp, blue-green curve, trying to see even the place where the thin envelope of atmosphere and the solid Earth meet, the curious word "fragile" comes to mind. To be on Earth and think of it as fragile is ridiculous, but to see it from out there and compare it with the deadness of the Moon!

Astronaut John Caffrey

The Greenhouse Effect

Background

Greenhouses are made almost completely of glass for two reasons. First, glass allows the maximum amount of sunlight into the building. Plants need the sunlight for photosynthesis. Second, glass prevents heat produced in the greenhouse from escaping. Clear plastic can serve these same two functions. When materials like glass and plastic let sunlight, but not heat, pass through them, the effect has come to be known as the **greenhouse effect**, which is a form of solar heating. How does the greenhouse effect work?

Visible light is only one form of light. Radiant heat is **infrared light**, another form. When visible light (sunlight) passes through the glass of a greenhouse, it strikes the objects in the building and its energy is absorbed. These objects begin to heat up. As they heat up, they give off radiant heat—infrared light. While visible light can pass through the glass of the greenhouse, the infrared light cannot. This means that the heat given off by objects in the greenhouse is trapped in the building. Therefore, even on cold, *sunny* days, the building can stay warm.

Some gases are like the glass of a greenhouse in that they trap heat. Several of these gases, including carbon dioxide (CO_2), water vapor (H_2O), nitrogen oxide (NO), and methane (CH_4), are present in Earth's atmosphere. The amounts of these gases are increasing daily because of some human activities such as driving cars and burning fuel, and because of such natural processes as decomposition in swamps, where methane is released into the atmosphere from the decomposition of dead plants and animals. At present, the atmosphere traps only a small part of the heat given off by the surface of Earth. As the amount of carbon dioxide and methane increases, however, Earth may become more like a greenhouse, growing warmer as the atmosphere traps more heat.

This activity will model how a greenhouse effect can occur.

Procedure

1. About 2 cm from the top of each plastic cup, use the hole punch to make a hole big enough for a thermometer to be inserted.

2. Fill each cup with dirt until the dirt is about 2.5 cm below the hole just made.

Objective

The objective of this activity is to observe and to investigate a model of how light and the atmosphere interact to make Earth suitable for life.

Materials

For each group of students:

◊ two large disposable plastic cups

◊ dirt to fill each cup

◊ something to prop up thermometers (a slightly smaller cup or stack of books will work)

◊ one rubber band

◊ two Celsius thermometers

◊ hole punch

3. Insert a thermometer through each hole so that the bulb is about 2.5 cm above the dirt and centered near the middle of the cup (see figure 1). ***Caution: Do not force the thermometer through the hole. If it will not go, punch a bigger hole.***

4. Turn the thermometers so that they can be read.

5. Cover one cup with plastic wrap, and leave the other cup uncovered. Secure the plastic wrap on the cup with a rubber band. The final arrangement should look like figure 1.

6. On a sunny day, take the two cups outside at the beginning of the class period, and place them where they will not be disturbed. Stabilize the thermometers so they will not move.

FIGURE 1

7. Record the initial temperature on each thermometer in the Data Table.

8. Record temperatures every 5 minutes for 30 minutes. During the first five minutes, write a prediction of what you think will happen to the temperatures of the two cups and give a reason for your prediction. Do this in the space below the Data Table.

9. Make a graph for the temperatures in each cup on a sheet of graph paper. Graph the temperatures on the vertical scale and the elapsed time on the horizontal scale. Designate each line as representing either the covered or the uncovered cup.

Questions and Conclusions

1. This activity is a model of what happens on Earth. What do the dirt and plastic wrap represent in this model?

2. What did you predict would happen?

3. Do your graphs support your prediction?

4. How does what you observed in each cup compare with your prediction? If the two are different, how can you account for this?

Time (min.)	Temperature of covered cup (° C)	Temperature of uncovered cup (° C)	Other observations
0			
5			
10			
15			
20			
25			
30			
35			
Total difference in temperature			

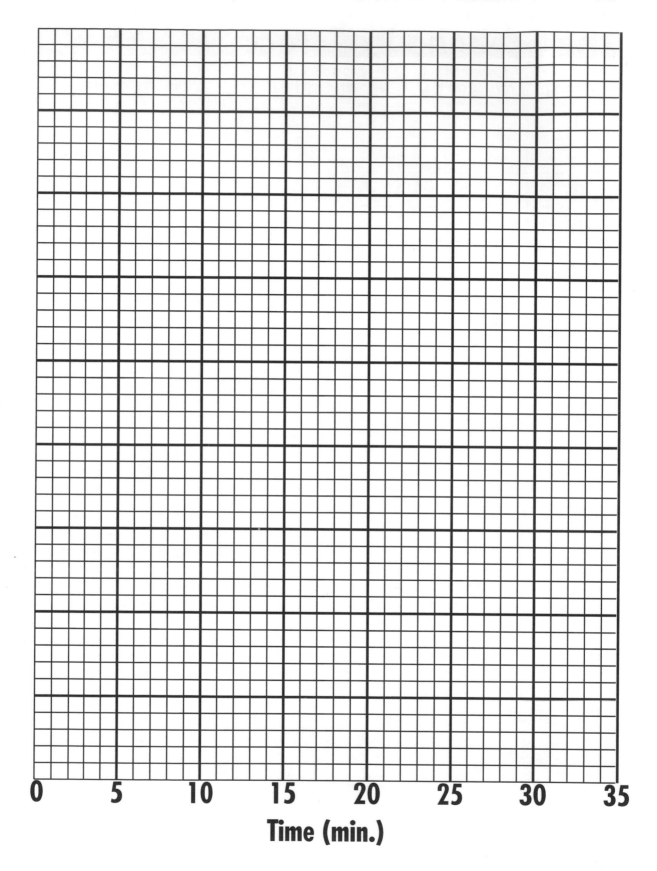

Temperature (°C)

Time (min.)

The Greenhouse Effect

What Is Happening?

The term **greenhouse effect** refers to the fact that visible light can pass through glass uninhibited but **infrared light** (heat) essentially cannot. The term was coined because this effect is most evident in greenhouses. The phenomenon is a consequence of the nature and behavior of light.

Light takes the form of X-rays, gamma rays, ultraviolet light, infrared light, radio waves, and microwaves—not just visible light. As objects in a greenhouse absorb light, they heat up and give off infrared light. While visible light can pass through the glass of the greenhouse, the infrared light cannot and it is reflected back in. So the heat given off by objects in the greenhouse stays in the greenhouse.

Some gases in Earth's atmosphere, notably carbon dioxide (CO_2), water vapor (H_2O) and methane (CH_4), act like the glass in a greenhouse. Sunlight passes through the atmosphere, strikes the ground, and the ground begins to heat up. The ground then gives off infrared light, which CO_2, H_2O, and CH_4 partially block from escaping the atmosphere. There has always been a natural and beneficial greenhouse effect operating on Earth due primarily to naturally occurring CO_2 and H_2O. The problem now is that human activities such as burning fossil fuels, which releases extra CO_2 into the atmosphere, and deforestation, which eliminates flora that use CO_2 from the atmosphere for photosynthesis, are disturbing the natural balance. As the quantities of these gases grow in the atmosphere they will prevent more and more of the heat from escaping—which may cause the temperature of Earth to rise.

Important Points for Students to Understand

◊ Light comes in many forms, not just the visible form which we can see.

◊ The passage or transmittance of the infrared light (heat) is inhibited by certain things, among them glass, CO_2, H_2O, and CH_4.

◊ CO_2, H_2O, and CH_4 only partially inhibit the passage of heat. The greater the concentration of the gas, the less heat is allowed through.

Materials

For the class:

◊ one large bag of potting soil

◊ one box of plastic wrap

◊ graph paper for each student

For each group of students:

◊ two large disposable plastic cups

◊ dirt to fill each cup

◊ something to prop up thermometers (a slightly smaller cup or stack of books will work)

◊ one rubber band

◊ two thermometers

◊ hole punch

Vocabulary

Greenhouse effect: A planet's atmospheric layers act like the glass of a greenhouse, permitting sunlight to pass through and strike a planet's surface but partially prohibiting the escape of heat (infrared light) radiated from that surface. As a result, the atmosphere warms up.

Infrared light: Heat or a form of electromagnetic radiation (light) which has a wavelength ranging from 1 μm to 1 mm. The wavelength of visible light is between 100 and 1,000 times shorter than infrared.

Radiant heat: Infrared light.

Time Management

This activity should take only one class period, but it will take the entire period. You may want to give the students assignments to complete between temperature readings. Time can be saved by having the students set up their cups the day before the activity is to be done. It is important to remember that the success of this activity depends on having a sunny day but not necessarily a warm day.

Preparation

Prior to preparing the cups, place all the materials in a central location so that students can easily obtain them. Keep track of the weather report and pick out a sunny day on which to do the activity.

Reading 8, entitled "After the Warming" is a concise overview of the greenhouse effect. It includes a description of the phenomenon, some of the research that has been done on it, and a synopsis of opposing views about global warming. Also refer to Reading 10, "The Greenhouse Effect;" and Reading 11, "Grand Theme 4: Interaction of Human Activities with the Natural Environment."

Suggestions for Further Study

Students may want to see what happens if the cups are left out all day long. Do the temperatures continue to rise? If not, why not, and how does this relate to Earth?

This is an excellent place for students to investigate what happens on other planets with regard to the greenhouse effect. Venus and Mars are especially good to research. Students will almost certainly want to know what will happen if the greenhouse effect increases dramatically on Earth. Venus provides a model of what might occur.

Finally, students may want to look into the research that is being done on the greenhouse effect and global warming. This is a controversial topic even in the scientific arena. Have students investigate the human activities that have led to an increase in carbon dioxide in the atmosphere.

Suggestions for Interdisciplinary Reading and Study

The oceans play a major role in moderating the amount of carbon dioxide in the atmosphere. The gas is dissolved in the ocean and eventually becomes a part of some shells and ocean sediments. Students can investigate research that is being done on the role of the ocean in carbon dioxide regulation.

The greenhouse effect and global warming are societal as well as environmental problems. Solutions based on environmental concerns alone are incomplete. Industrialized societies depend heavily on burning fossil fuels, the chief source of carbon dioxide in the atmosphere. Solutions to these problems must take into account societal and technological factors as well as environmental ones. What would be the impact on the United States and other industrialized countries of shifting away from fossil fuels? What technology would be required to do this? Are there other possible solutions besides alternative energy sources?

Answers to Questions for Students

1. The dirt represents the surface of Earth. The plastic wrap represents Earth's atmosphere.

2. Predictions may vary slightly. Pay careful attention to what students predict—it will provide clues for what misconceptions exist in your class and give you guidance about whether to extend this activity.

    The temperature in both cups should have increased, but at different rates. As the dirt in each cup gives off heat, the temperature of each increases. In the covered cup, however, the heat does not escape so the temperature rises more rapidly.

3. The students should see a graphical representation of the answer to question 2.

4. Answers will vary.

Quote from Space

The sight of the ice particles in front of the Shuttle is like . . . fireflies. They're different colors. Some of those sparkles out there are red . . . most of them are white . . . some really bright ones out there. And as the Sun sets on the orbiter, the ice crystals go out. The last few of them turn red. Then they're all red. Then they're gone.

When you look outside and see the black of space and the ice crystals following us around and the sunrise and sunset every hour-and-a-half; [you] look out and see the lightning storms flashing, the cities making their light patterns beneath the clouds, the patterns in the ocean, flying over the Himalayas as we do the last orbits tonight, then I know I'm really in space.

Astronaut Jeff Hoffman

Creature Feature

Objective

The objective of this activity is to consider some of the characteristics of Venus and Mars which make the planets uninhabitable for life as we know it.

Materials

◊ construction paper (at least three different colors)

◊ scissors

◊ glue

◊ aluminum foil

◊ straws

◊ toothpicks

◊ paper cups

◊ transparent tape

◊ floral wire

Background

For as long as we have known that there are other planets in the Solar System, we have wondered if there might be life on them and if they might support human life. The planet that has received most of this attention is Mars. Some surface features of Mars which are visible from Earth have in the past led us to believe that entire civilizations may have once existed there. In 1976 Viking I and II actually landed on Mars and collected soil samples for analysis. The results of these tests did not support the belief that life may have existed on Mars.

Mars and Venus are Earth's closest neighbors. The differences between them are striking. In many ways, Earth can be thought of as the happy medium between the two extremes that Mars and Venus represent. We are aware of many of the forms of life, both plant and animal, that exist on Earth. Imagine that you were able to create an organism that could survive on Venus or Mars. Would it resemble a plant or animal that you are familiar with? What features would it need for life on these planets? In order to answer these questions, you will need to become more familiar with the characteristics of Earth's next door neighbors, Venus and Mars.

Procedure

1. Carefully read and study the following brief descriptions of Venus and Mars.

VENUS

Venus is the second planet from the Sun between Mercury and Earth. Because it is closer to the Sun than Earth, the sunlight that strikes it is almost twice as intense as that which strikes Earth. The Venusian atmosphere is 96 percent carbon dioxide. This high concentration of carbon dioxide results in a runaway greenhouse effect (see Activity 8) such that the surface temperature on Venus is 477° C. The atmosphere is much "thicker" than Earth's, so much so that the air pressure at the surface of the planet is 90 times that on Earth. It is so thick that only about 25 percent of the sunlight that strikes it passes through to the surface; the remaining 75 percent is reflected to space. Consequently there is a constant eerie, reddish light at the surface of the planet during the day.

The Venusian atmosphere has no oxygen to speak of. It is filled with clouds made of sulfuric acid, a very corrosive substance. The planet rotates slowly compared to Earth. One day on Venus is as long as 117 days on Earth. The surface of Venus is similar to Earth's in composition and density, and Venus is only 5 percent smaller than Earth. Venus is considered more similar to Earth than any other planet in the Solar System.

MARS

Mars, the next planet beyond Earth, is similar to Earth in several ways as well. The tilt of its rotational axis and its rotational speed are almost identical to Earth's. So the Martian day is about the same length as Earth's, and Mars has seasons like Earth. The Martian atmosphere is very thin. The air pressure at the surface is 166 times less than that on Earth. Carbon dioxide constitutes 95 percent of this atmosphere, but unlike Venus there is no substantial green-house effect. So the planet is subject to a wide range of temperatures. The temperature can be as low as −128° C or as high as 37° C during a Martian summer. At the north and south poles, the temperatures remain cold enough year-round to maintain permanent ice caps made of frozen carbon dioxide. The atmospheric pressure on Mars is far too low to allow the existence of liquid water. It is believed that what water does exist on Mars is frozen either beneath the polar ice caps or in clouds. The surface of Mars is exten-sively covered with iron oxide (rust) giving the planet its characteristic red color.

2. In your group, design and construct a model of some form of life that could survive on Venus. Be sure to include features that are capable of handling the conditions on Venus as described above.

3. Repeat step 2 for Mars.

4. In your group prepare an explanation of the features of both organisms and designate one or two people in the group to present this to the class.

Questions and Conclusions

1. What features of Venus make it most unlikely that humans or other forms of life from Earth could survive there?

2. What features of Mars make it most unlikely that humans or other forms of life from Earth could survive there?

3. Could the "life form" that you designed for Venus survive on Earth? Why or why not?

4. Could the "life form" that you designed for Mars survive on Earth? Why or why not?

Creature Feature

Materials

For each group of students:

◊ construction paper (at least three different colors)

◊ scissors

◊ glue

◊ aluminum foil

◊ straws

◊ toothpicks

◊ paper cups

◊ transparent tape

◊ floral wire

What Is Happening?

The purpose of this activity is to help students understand and appreciate the fact that Earth is the only planet in the Solar System that sustains life. With the age of space exploration came the realization that we may one day be able to travel to other planets in the Solar System and the realization that these planets are uninhabitable. Neither the Soviet nor the U.S. missions to Mars and Venus, the planets closest to Earth, have succeeded in finding signs of life past or present on either planet. In this activity, students will consider some of the conditions on Venus and Mars that make these findings plausible. Hopefully, in the course of the activity they will come to appreciate the uniqueness of Earth and learn the importance of stewardship toward the planet.

"Creature Feature" is well-suited to cooperative learning groups. It is strongly suggested that each group be required to present their creatures to the entire class and explain them.

Important Points for Students to Understand

◊ Earth is the only planet in the Solar System that sustains life.

◊ Through space exploration, we are now aware of specific conditions on Mars and Venus that make the planets uninhabitable.

Time Management

This activity will require at least one class period for groups to construct and present their creatures to the rest of the class. More time will be required for class and teacher critiques of the creatures.

Preparation

Be sure to have at least the materials listed above on hand, but try to have even more. The more materials the students have to work with, the more creative their creatures will be. You may want to prepare in advance a rating scheme so that classes can vote on the best creature for Mars and Venus. If the criteria are made known to the students, it may help them to design creatures that directly relate to the conditions on Mars and Venus. It is a good idea to prepare some way to display all the groups' creatures for the entire class. One suggestion is to hang them from the ceiling.

For further information, refer to Reading 9, "Grand Theme 2: Atmosphere, Oceans, Cryosphere, and Hydrologic Cycle;" and Reading 11, "Grand Theme 4: Interaction of Human Activities with the Natural Environment."

Suggestions for Further Study

Earth's conditions and its life forms are interrelated—each impacts the other. For instance, it is believed that as plants developed, they removed some carbon dioxide from the atmosphere and increased the amount of oxygen there. This made conditions more hospitable for other forms of life. We know that human activity is altering the composition of the atmosphere. As an extension to this activity, it would be interesting to have the students consider how their creatures might change the conditions on Venus and on Mars by their existence.

Encourage students to investigate what changes would be necessary to make Mars habitable. Some scientists have suggested that if all the carbon dioxide frozen in the Martian polar ice caps were in the atmosphere, there might be a sufficient greenhouse effect to make the existence of liquid water possible.

NASA has published a seven-volume series under the title *Space Science in the Twenty-First Century: Imperatives for the Decades 1995 to 2015*. The volume titled "Mission to Planet Earth" contains much more detail on planetary comparisons and on those factors which have made life possible on Earth.

Suggestions for Interdisciplinary Reading and Study

This activity is most appropriate at the end of the astronomy unit as some of the concepts that are used in the descriptions of Mars and Venus, particularly seasons and the greenhouse effect, are covered earlier in the unit. Alternatively, the activity could be used in the study of life science once the relevant concepts from astronomy are understood. As the students' understanding of life science grows, so will their understanding of the severity of the conditions for life on Mars and Venus. Used in this way, the activity could serve as a type of pre-and post-assessment to allow

the students' increased understanding of astronomy and life science to be reflected in their "creature" designs.

Answers to Questions for Students

1. Lack of liquid water, lack of oxygen in atmosphere, high surface temperature, and high atmospheric pressure, among others.

2. Lack of liquid water, lack of oxygen in atmosphere, low surface temperature, low atmospheric pressure, global dust storms, among others.

3. Answers will depend on the students' models.

4. Same as 3.

Seasons

Winter touches each tree branch,
With icy fingers so very cold.
Suddenly spring comes along
Which will dispel winter's hold.

When summer first approaches,
Balmy breezes will be at play.
Then soon heat and humidity
Will be around awhile to stay.

Autumn's red and golden colors,
Warn us winter is very near,
And so much can be seen
In each season of the year.

Evelyn Nitso

Reason for the Seasons

Background

Many drawings of Earth's orbit around the Sun look like figure 1. These are meant to give you a view of a nearly circular orbit seen from the side. Rather than a circle, the shape of the orbit in figure 1 is called an ellipse. Often, however, students mistakenly think that such drawings show Earth's *true* orbit.

While it is true that Earth does have a slightly elliptical orbit, it is not nearly as extreme as that illustrated in figure 1. That picture makes it look like Earth is much closer to the Sun at some times and much farther away at others. Actually, Earth's orbit looks much more like a circle than an ellipse. Figure 2 is a much more accurate representation of Earth's orbit around the Sun.

Many people think that the reason Earth has seasons is because its orbit looks like figure 1. They think that when Earth is closest to the Sun, summer occurs, and when it is farthest from the Sun, we have winter. If distance from the Sun determined the seasons, then it should be summer in the southern hemisphere (Argentina, for example) when it is summer in the northern hemisphere (the United States or England), but this is not what happens. When it is summer in the northern hemisphere, it is winter in the southern hemisphere.

The reason Earth has seasons is because of the angle at which it rotates as it revolves around the Sun. Most objects rotate around an axis that is straight up and down, just like when someone spins a ball on his or her finger. But Earth's axis is tilted, as shown in figure 3, and this tilt causes the seasons.

Objective

The objective of this activity is to understand why Earth has seasons.

(Not to scale)

FIGURE 1

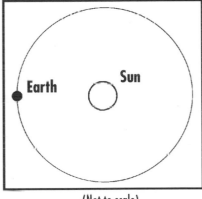

(Not to scale)

FIGURE 2

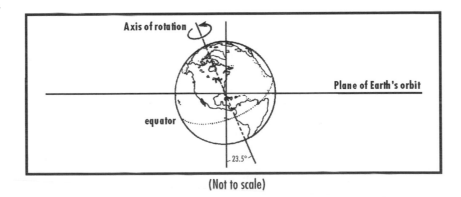

(Not to scale)

FIGURE 3

Procedure

1. Arrange the lamp and globe(s) as shown in figure 4. If you are using two globes, be sure that each is the same distance from the lamp. A minimum distance of 1.5 m from the bulb is recommended.

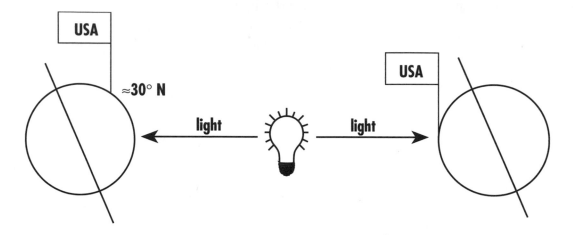

2. Darken the room.

3. Make and record observations about the intensity of light on the different parts of the globe that are facing the light.

4. Take one globe and walk it through an orbit around the Sun, making sure that you maintain the tilt of the axis and keep it oriented in the same direction. At each position, you may want to spin the globe so that the difference from day and night can be observed.

5. Make and record observations about the brightness of light on the United States as the globe goes through its orbit.

Questions and Conclusions

1. How did the brightness of light on the United States compare in the first demonstration when there was a globe on each side of the light?

2. How can you account for the differences in the brightness of light?

3. How did the brightness of light on the United States change when the globe was walked around the Sun?

4. At what points in the orbit do you think each of the seasons would occur?

5. When it is summer in the United States, where might it be winter?

6. Do the seasons in other parts of the United States differ from the seasons where you live? Why or why not?

7. If you traveled to Australia right now, what season would it be? Explain.

8. What would be necessary for other planets to have seasons as Earth does?

Reason for the Seasons

Materials

For the class:

◊ one or two globes mounted so that the axis of rotation is tilted to 23.5° from vertical

◊ a bright light source (lamp with at least a 75-watt bulb and without a shade)

Vocabulary

Orbit: The path followed by one body revolving about another body.

Ellipse: An oval; a closed curve in which the sum of the distances from two fixed points to any point on the curve is constant.

Axis: A straight line about which a figure or body is symmetrical.

Rotation axis: A straight line around which a body rotates.

What Is Happening?

Earth travels around the Sun in a slightly elliptical orbit. Because of this orbit, Earth's distance from the Sun varies slightly depending on where Earth is in its orbit. Contrary to popular opinion, however, Earth's seasons are only slightly related to this small variation in the planet's distance from the Sun. This is one of the most common misconceptions in astronomy. Mistakenly, people think that when Earth is farthest away from the Sun, it is winter; and when Earth is closest, summer occurs. The change in distance is, in fact, not great enough to cause any significant change in temperature. As a matter of fact, Earth is closest to the Sun in January, when it is winter in the Northern Hemisphere. Furthermore, if distance from the Sun determined the seasons, then all of Earth should have the same season at the same time. This is not the case. When it is summer in the Northern Hemisphere, it is winter in the Southern Hemisphere.

Instead, the reason Earth has seasons has to do with the angle at which Earth rotates as it revolves around the Sun. Generally, when objects rotate, they rotate around a vertical axis, just like a spinning top or a basketball spinning on someone's finger. Earth, however, rotates around an axis tilted relative to its orbit. The angle of the tilt is 23.5° from vertical (see figure 5).

Due to this tilt of Earth's rotation axis, some parts of Earth receive more vertical rays of Sunlight and others receive more slanting rays. Slanting rays of sunlight are less intense and do not cause as much heating as more vertical rays of sunlight. In summer in the Northern Hemisphere, the north pole is tilted toward the Sun, as shown in figure 6. This arrangement allows for the more vertical rays of sunlight to strike the Northern Hemisphere and, therefore, the United States.

In winter, the direction of tilt is the same as in summer, but since Earth is now on the opposite side of the Sun, the Southern Hemisphere is tilted toward the Sun and the Northern Hemisphere is tilted away (see figure 7). The rays that

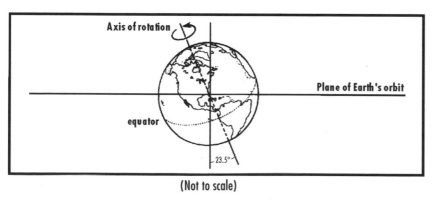

Axis of rotation

Plane of Earth's orbit

equator

23.5°

(Not to scale)

FIGURE 5 Tilt of Earth's Rotational Axis

NATIONAL SCIENCE TEACHERS ASSOCIATION

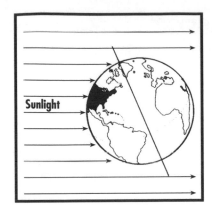

FIGURE 6
Summer in the Northern Hemisphere

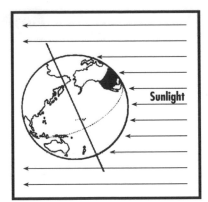

FIGURE 7
Winter in the Northern Hemishpere

strike the Northern Hemisphere are more slanting and do not cause as much heating. Fall and spring are simply the points between these two extremes.

Another consequence of having a tilted axis is that the day's length varies throughout the year. This further contributes to seasonal temperatures; the longer the day, the more energy received from the Sun to warm the atmosphere and the less time for that warmth to dissipate.

This explains seasonal temperature variations, but day-to-day changes are moderated by Earth's atmosphere. That is why the hottest and coldest days of the year rarely occur on the summer and winter solstices, respectively.

Important Points for Students to Understand

◊ Earth's distance from the Sun has little to do with the seasons.

◊ The seasons are caused by Earth's axis of rotation being tilted 23.5° from the vertical with respect to its orbital plane.

◊ When a hemisphere is tilted toward the Sun, summer occurs, and when it is tilted away from the Sun, winter occurs there.

◊ Earth's orbit is only slightly elliptical; not nearly as elliptical as most people think.

◊ Slanting rays of sunlight do not heat the surface of Earth as much as vertical rays of sunlight.

Time Management

This demonstration should take less than half a class period.

Preparation

Misconceptions can be very hard to correct in students. One strategy for addressing misconceptions is making the students aware of their own ideas. This can be accomplished in the activity by having the students write out their understanding of why seasons occur before doing the activity. This serves three purposes. First, it gains the students' attention. Second, it makes them aware of their own beliefs. Finally, it provides a resource to help the teacher focus instruction on misconceptions that the students identify.

In this activity, one or two globes and a bright light are used to demonstrate why the seasons occur. Be sure that the light source is operable.

For further information, refer to Reading 12, "Reason for the Seasons."

Suggestions for Further Study

Most textbooks depict Earth's orbit as much more elliptical than it actually is. Students could plot a scale model of Earth's true orbit to see that it more closely resembles a circle than an ellipse. This would enable them to see that distance is not a factor in the seasons. Include instructions on how to draw ellipses of varying eccentricity.

Students may also be interested in trying to devise a more graphic way of explaining the reason Earth has seasons. It would be informative for them to study other planets to learn if they have seasons.

Suggestions for Interdisciplinary Reading and Study

Seasons are a common theme in music, literature, and art. Encourage students to find all kinds of music (classical, popular, folk) that have references to the seasons. The poem "Winter Moon" (at the beginning of Activity 11) by Langston Hughes provides a bridge from astronomy to meteorology. Ask the students what changes occur in the atmosphere from season to season to make the Moon appear different. In many locations, winter air is much less humid than at other times, making for a much sharper image of the Moon. The poem "Seasons" (at the beginning of this activity) by Evelyn Nitso provides a description of each season.

Answers to Questions for Students

1. The light should have been brighter on the United States on the globe which had the United States tilted toward the Sun. In the diagram for the procedure section for this activity, this would be the globe on the right.

2. When the United States is tilted away from the light (the Sun), it receives more slanting rays of sunlight, and the light is therefore not as intense.

3. As the globe was walked around the light, the students should have observed a cycle of increasing and then decreasing intensity depending on where the globe was originally positioned in the orbit.

4. Winter and summer occur on opposite sides of the light when the intensity of light on the United States is the dimmest and brightest respectively. Fall and spring occur on opposite sides of the light half-way between winter and summer.

5. Somewhere in the Southern Hemisphere. Chile, for example.

6. Yes. For example, winter in the northeastern part of the United States is much longer and colder than in the southeast. This is because the farther north and south from the equator, the shorter the winter days are.

7. Depends on the present season. Generally, it would be the opposite of what the season is in the United States. If it is spring in the United States, it would be fall in Australia. This is because Australia is in the Southern Hemisphere and the United States is in the Northern Hemisphere.

8. They would have to have a tilt in their axes of rotation just as Earth has. It would not have to be a 23.5° tilt, however.

Winter Moon

How thin and sharp is the moon tonight!
How thin and sharp and ghostly white
Is the slim curved crook of the moon tonight!

Langston Hughes

Ping-Pong Phases

Background

Every 29.5 days the Moon goes through a predictable cycle of changes in its shape which we call **phases**. For thousands of years, people have recorded these phases and during this time, the cycle has never changed. Even though it is known with great accuracy what the Moon will look like on any night of the year, many people cannot explain why the Moon's shape appears to change. Some people say that Earth's shadow falls on the Moon and blocks our view of part of it, as shown in figure 1. Others say that clouds block part of the Moon. Both explanations are incorrect.

Actually, the physical shape of the Moon never changes. It is always a sphere with millions of craters and other landforms on it. What changes is the portion of the Moon that can be seen from Earth. Half of the Moon is always illuminated by the Sun. Sometimes, the entire illuminated part of the Moon can be seen from Earth; this is called a full Moon. Other times, none of the illuminated part can be seen—a new Moon. And all the stages in between a new and full Moon occur as well. But why does the shape of the Moon appear to change in this way? It is because the Moon is in orbit around Earth.

This activity will show how the Moon's orbit causes the Moon's phases.

Objective

The objective of this activity is to understand the cause of the Moon's phases.

Materials for Part 1

◊ 1 bright lamp (at least 75-watt) without shade

◊ 1 extension cord

◊ 1 Ping-Pong ball for each student

Materials for Part 2

For each pair of students:

◊ cardboard

◊ 15-cm diameter Styrofoam ball

◊ pencil

◊ black paint suitable for Styrofoam

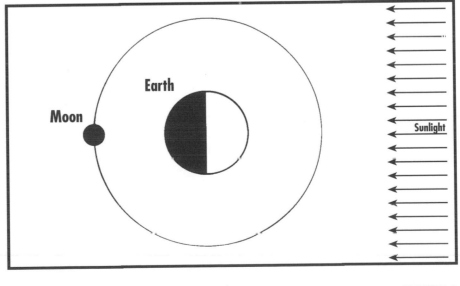

(Not to scale)

FIGURE 1

Part I Procedure

1. Place the bright lamp without a lamp shade in the center of a darkened room. Make the room as dark as possible, covering any major sources of stray light.

2. Each student should have a Ping-Pong ball (a Moon), and the entire class should form a circle around the lamp. This circle should be as tight as possible but still allow each student to turn around with one arm extended. (Two circles, each with their own lamp, would work better if there are more than 15 students in the class.)

3. Everyone should face the lamp (the Sun) and hold the ball directly in front of his or her body and slightly above his or her head.

4. Observe what portion of the side of the "Moon" facing you is illuminated by the "Sun."

5. Now turn 45° to the left and make the same observation.

6. Continue to make 45° turns until you are once again facing the "Sun."

Questions and Conclusions

1. How much of the illuminated part of the ball (Moon) could you see when you were facing the lamp (Sun)?

2. How much of the illuminated part of the Moon could you see after each turn?

3. Whether you could see it or not, how much of the ball's surface area was always illuminated?

Part 2 Procedure

1. Paint exactly half of the Styrofoam ball black with paint. The simplest way to do this is to cut a hole the diameter of the ball in a piece of cardboard. Putting the ball in that hole before painting it will keep one side protected from the paint. This simulates the Moon with one side illuminated by the Sun and the other side facing away from the Sun, the "dark side" of the Moon. (The Moon is actually all about the same color.)

2. Stick a pencil about 5 cm into the Styrofoam ball as shown in figure 2.

3. Stand in an open space and have another student stand about 3 m away facing you and holding the ball at eye level so that *you* can see the *black* side only.

4. The student holding the "Moon" should walk around you in a circle, making sure not to turn the ball and to always face in the same direction; for example, always face the board. The student will have to walk backwards and sideways at times to do this.

5. At each of the eight positions indicated on the Data Sheet, draw the portion of the white part of the ball that you can see.

6. Switch places with the student helping you and repeat the activity.

7. Label your drawings on the Data Sheet with a name for each phase of the Moon.

FIGURE 2

Data Sheet

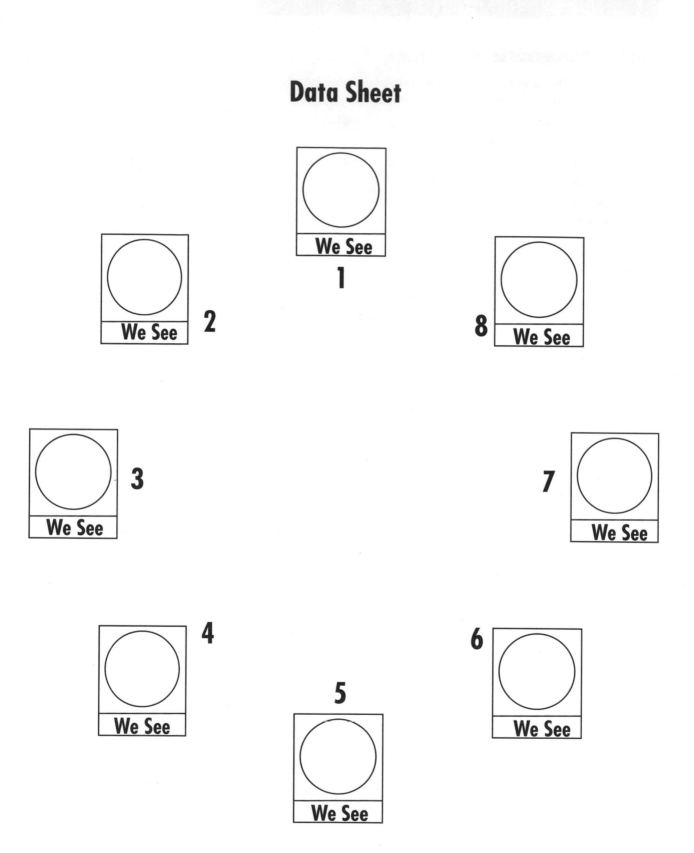

Keep this page upright as you draw what you see.

Questions and Conclusions

4. What fraction of the ball was white (illuminated by the Sun) during the whole activity?

5. Were you able to see all the white or "illuminated" portion of the ball throughout the activity?

6. Describe what happened to the white portion of the ball that you could see as the Moon went around you in a circle.

7. If you represent Earth and the ball represents the Moon, describe where in the room the Sun would have been.

Ping-Pong Phases

Materials for Part 1

◊ 1 bright lamp (at least 75-watt) without shade

◊ 1 extension cord

◊ 1 Ping-Pong ball for each student

Materials for Part 2

For each pair of students:

◊ cardboard

◊ 15-cm diameter Styrofoam ball

◊ pencil

◊ black paint suitable for Styrofoam

Vocabulary

Phases of the Moon: The cycle of changes of the portion of the Moon that is visible from Earth.

What Is Happening?

Every 29.5 days, the Moon goes through a predictable cycle of changes. While most people are well aware of the Moon's phases, one of the most common misconceptions in astronomy concerns why these changes in its apparent shape occur. Perhaps the most prevalent, *incorrect* explanation for Moon phases is that they are caused by Earth's shadow on the Moon. (This is an eclipse.) Another incorrect explanation is that clouds block part of the Moon.

The *correct* explanation of the phases of the Moon involves visualizing the relationship among three separate objects, two of which are in motion around the third. Models work best to explain and to visualize this relationship. Figure 3 shows one model of how the Sun, Earth, and Moon interact to produce the phases of the Moon. In this model the Sun is positioned off the right hand side of the page. The inner ring of Moons illustrates that half of the Moon is always illuminated—the half facing the Sun. However, depending on where the Moon is in its orbit around Earth, we may see all of the illuminated area, none of it, or any fraction between the two. The outer ring of Moons shows how the Moon would appear in each of eight positions to a person on Earth.

FIGURE 3

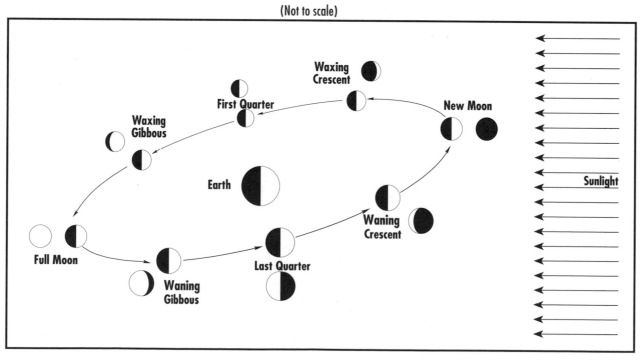

(Not to scale)

(Not to scale)

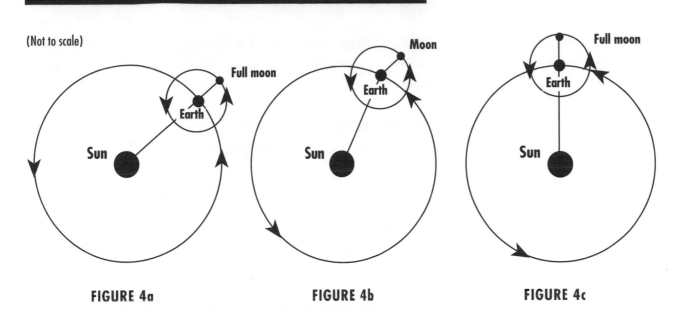

FIGURE 4a　　　　　　**FIGURE 4b**　　　　　　**FIGURE 4c**

This cycle of apparent shapes repeats every 29.5 days. This period of time may seem incorrect since it takes the Moon only 27.3 days to go around Earth once. The difference is explained by the fact that Earth is moving too. Figure 4a-c illustrates this. Figure 4a shows the alignment of the Sun, Moon, and Earth during the full Moon. After 27.3 days, the Moon has made one complete orbit around Earth, but Earth has moved in its own orbit too. Because of this, it takes about two more days before the Moon is back in a position relative to Earth to appear full. At that point, the cycle of phases begins again.

This activity is designed to show that the reason for the changes in the visible shape of the Moon is the motion of the Moon around Earth. Some students will probably question why an eclipse does not occur once a month when the Moon is on the opposite side of Earth from the Sun. The plane of the Moon's orbit is slightly tilted (as shown in figure 5), this tilt precludes a monthly eclipse from occurring. It is important to help students make the connection between what happens in this activity and reality. Questions like "Where are the Sun, Moon, and Earth when the Moon is in the first quarter?" require them to transfer their thinking from the model to reality.

The cause of phases of the Moon is one of the toughest concepts to visualize and understand. We have included two simulations for students in this activity to help you reinforce their

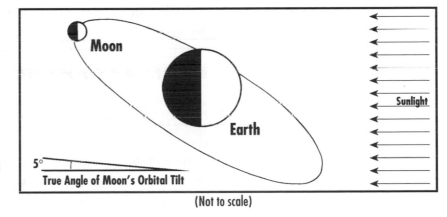

(Not to scale)

FIGURE 5　**The Tilted Plane of the Moon's Orbit**

thinking. Begin with Part 1 of this activity, then use Part 2 if you determine that some students are still clinging to naive conceptions.

Important Points for Students to Understand

◊ Half of the Moon is always illuminated.

◊ The actual shape of the Moon does not change, only the portion of it that can be seen from Earth.

◊ The cycle of changes in the visible shape of the Moon is due to the Moon orbiting Earth.

◊ The changes in the apparent shape of the Moon occur in a predictable cycle which repeats every 29.5 days.

◊ The same side of the Moon always faces Earth, but the same side is not always illuminated because the Moon rotates.

◊ The plane of the Moon's orbit is slightly tilted, and this precludes a monthly eclipse.

Time Management

Including set up, this activity should take one class period for each part.

Preparation for Part I

The misconceptions that students have about the phases of the Moon can be very difficult to change. Simply presenting the correct explanation is often not enough. One strategy that may prove helpful is increasing students' awareness of their own ideas about phases. Prior to the activity, ask the them to write their own explanation of why the shape of the Moon appears to change. Encourage them to use diagrams in their explanation. This exercise also serves the purpose of making the teacher aware of specific misconceptions that students may have. After completing the activity, you could return their original explanations for them to correct.

Prior to the class, be sure that there is one Ping-Pong ball for each student and that the lamp is in working order. It may be necessary to divide the class into two groups in order for them to stand close enough to the light and yet have enough room to rotate with one arm outstretched.

For further information, refer to Reading 13, "Phases of the Moon;" and Reading 14, "Understanding the Moon Illusion."

Preparation for Part 2

Painting the Styrofoam balls is a messy task, so you may want to do this for the students. Tempera or acrylic paint works best. Some spray paint dissolves Styrofoam. Only one class set needs to be prepared. They can then be used repeatedly.

Be sure beforehand that there is enough room for all students to work at once. It is helpful to mark off work spaces prior to the class. Students will work in pairs in this activity. You may want to pair students up prior to the class in order to save time.

It is important that students move the Styrofoam balls correctly when walking around the observer. One side of the Moon must always face in the same direction, toward a wall or the chalkboard, for example. The ball must *not* rotate. It is strongly suggested that you demonstrate the correct movement for the students. If done correctly, the larger size of the Styrofoam ball will allow students to understand how what they can see of the illuminated side of the Moon becomes the new, waxing, full, and waning Moon they see in the sky.

This activity may perpetuate some misconceptions that students already have about the Moon. You should point these out to the students and make it clear this activity is only a model which shows how a half-illuminated sphere may take on different appearances depending on the relative positions of the sphere and the observer. The students should be made to realize that this model is inaccurate in the following ways. First, the Moon is not varied in coloration as the Styrofoam ball is. Second, the same side of the Moon is not always illuminated. At different times in the cycle of phases, all parts of the Moon become illuminated. Finally, the Moon rotates as it orbits Earth whereas the Styrofoam ball in this activity does not. It is this rotation of the Moon that allows the same side of the Moon always to face Earth, and it allows all parts of the Moon to be illuminated at different times in the cycle.

Suggestions for Further Study

Students can use these activities to dispel two common misconceptions about the Moon. It is commonly believed that the same side of the Moon is always illuminated since the same side always faces Earth. The first activity best demonstrates that this is not true. Another misconception many people have is that since the same side of the Moon always faces Earth, the Moon must not rotate. From the first activity students can see that even though the same side of the Ping-Pong ball always faces them, the ball is

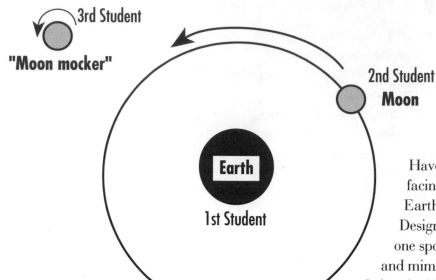

FIGURE 6

rotating nonetheless.

Care must be taken, if you choose Part 2, to not perpetuate these misconceptions.

Here is another short activity that may further help dispel these misconceptions. Have two students stand 2 m apart facing each other. One represents Earth and the other the Moon. Designate a third student to stand in one spot to the side of the other two and mimic the motion of the person being the Moon (see figure 6). Have the student representing the Moon walk side-step in a circle around the other student, facing him or her at all times. In this way, the same side of the student representing the Moon is always facing "Earth." As the "Moon" is going around "Earth," the third student stays in one spot but will have to turn his or her body in order to face the same way as the "Moon." This should demonstrate to students that even though the same side of the Moon always faces Earth, the Moon still rotates and hence the same side could not always be illuminated by the Sun.

Going beyond the concepts addressed directly, this activity is a good starting point for students to explore the difference between a lunar eclipse and a new Moon and to learn the names of the phases of the Moon. It is also an opportunity to discuss the moons of other planets.

Suggestions for Interdisciplinary Reading and Study

Through the ages, the phases of the Moon and lunar eclipses have been a source of myth and folklore. It is only in the last few centuries that phases and eclipses have been correctly explained. Different cultures have explained these phenomenon in different ways. Comparing these cultures and their explanations would be an interesting interdisciplinary project.

The phases of the Moon have also found their way into poetry. Langston Hughes's "Winter Moon" (at the beginning of this activity) and Myra Cohn Livingston's "Moon" (at the beginning of Activity 1) are two examples. Students may have heard or read the phrase "blue Moon." Encourage them to find out what it means when someone says that something happens "once in a blue Moon." ("Blue Moon" refers to the occurrence of two full moons in the same month, something that happens only once or twice a year.) Ask students to find specific references to the blue Moon in music and literature.

For many people, the Moon in all its phases is a thing of great beauty and wonder. As such, it has been the source of inspiration for art, literature, and music. Encourage students to listen for references to the Moon in their favorite music. Challenge them to find misconceptions about the Moon in these songs.

Answers to Questions for Students

1. None or almost none. This is the new Moon.

2. 1st turn—25 percent of the illuminated portion of the Moon was visible, corresponding to the waxing crescent phase.

    2nd turn—50 percent—first quarter

    3rd turn—75 percent—waxing gibbous

    4th turn—100 percent—full Moon

    5th turn—75 percent—waning gibbous

    6th turn —50 percent—third quarter

    7th turn—25 percent—waning crescent

    8th turn—0 percent—new Moon

3. Fifty percent of the ball was always illuminated.

4. Half of the ball was white even though it could not all be seen all the time.

5. No.

6. Assuming the student started with the black side facing him or her, none of the white would have been seen initially. As the Moon moved, a crescent would have first appeared, then a half, then three quarters, then a full Moon. As the Moon continued to move, this pattern would have reversed until only the black side was visible again.

7. This will vary for each student. The Sun should be in a position to illuminate the white half of the ball.

Introduction

The following readings elaborate on the concepts presented in the preceding activities. They include essays written especially for this volume, scientific articles, excerpts from other teacher materials, and excerpts from publications written by NASA. While these readings were written and selected with the teacher in mind, students should be encouraged to read them for interest and for additional study.

Angular Diameters

Measuring diameters of objects in the Solar System presents just as big a problem as measuring distances. Since we cannot measure the size directly, we use a technique that measures the **angular diameter**.

Figure 1 shows an example of an angular diameter. If you could take one piece of string and stretch it from where you are all the way to the right side of the Moon, and then stretch another piece of string to the left side of the

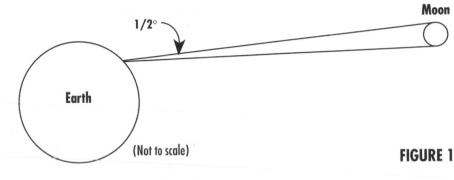

FIGURE 1

Moon from the same starting point, the angle between those two pieces of string would be $^1/_2$°.

It is possible for two objects to have the same angular diameter even if they are not the same size. Hold your thumb in front of one eye while closing the other. Move your thumb closer to your eye or farther away until it just blocks your view of someone else's head. You know that your thumb is not as big as the person's head, so how can your thumb block the view? The reason is that both your thumb and the person's head have the same angular diameter at that point where one blocks the other, even though they are not the same size. When two objects have the same angular diameter, they have the same *apparent size*; that is, they *appear* to be the same size. You will also notice that when your thumb is closer to your eyes, it appears larger than at arm's length.

The apparent size of an object relates to how close or far away it is. Take a coin and place it on a piece of paper. Make a pencil dot seven centimeters to the left of the coin. Draw two lines that go from the dot to either side of the coin as shown in figure 2.

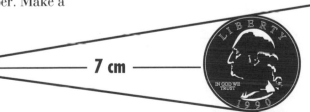

FIGURE 2

Now move the coin about a centimeter to the right and draw the two lines again from the same point. Move the coin further to the right and draw the lines. Notice that as the coin is moved farther away, the angle gets smaller. If you viewed the coin from the dot, the apparent size would continually decrease.

Angular diameters are only useful if the distance to the object is known. An object's true diameter can be calculated from its distance and its angular diameter by two different methods. One method involves using an equation from geometry—$s = r(q/57)$ where:

s = true diameter of the object
r = distance to the object (must be in same unit as "s")
q = angular diameter of the object in degrees
57 = conversion factor of radians to degrees

This is true for small angles. Unfortunately, the angular diameter of most objects of interest in astronomy, including planets, is $^1/_2$° or less, and such angles are hard to measure with commonly available equipment. The second method does not require expensive equipment but does require knowledge of similar triangles.

The relevant features of similar triangles can be illustrated with the following exercise. Using a protractor, draw two lines on a piece of paper to make an acute angle (the angle in figure 3 is 53°). On one line, start at the point of intersection and make a mark every 3 cm for 12 cm. On the other line, start at the same point and make a dot every 5 cm for 15 cm. Connect the dots as shown in figure 3. You have now made a series of triangles that all have one angle in common, angle X. In this diagram, angle X is 53°. Measure angles A, B, and C in your drawing using a protractor. Are they the same? Measure angles D, E, and F. Are they the same? When all the corresponding angles are equal like this, then the triangles are similar. Similar triangles have another interesting feature. Measure lines XD and XE and divide the first by the second. Now measure lines DA and EB and divide the first by the second. You should get the same, or nearly the same, answer for both. This feature of similar triangles is essential in using angular diameters to determine true diameters of planets in the Solar System.

Figure 4 shows how a dime and the principles of similar triangles can be used to calculate the diameter of the Moon. Once the dime is moved to a point where it just blocks out the view of the full Moon, the two have the same angular diameter. Since

FIGURE 3

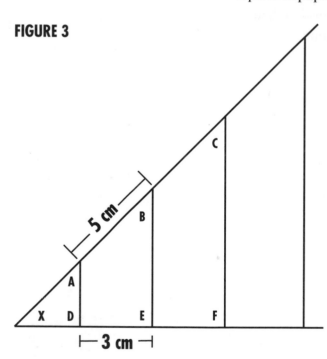

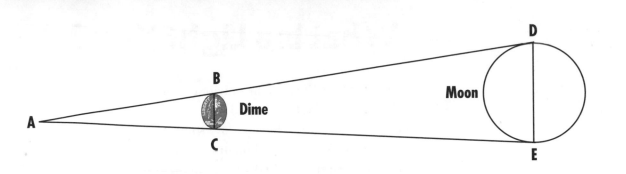

they have the same angular diameter, two similar triangles exist, ABC and ADE. The distance to the dime (AB) and its diameter (BC) are easily measured. The distance to the Moon (AD) is known from past measurements. Therefore the diameter of the Moon (DE) can be calculated by solving the ratio AB/AD = BC/DE for DE. Again, this is possible because of the similar triangles which exist when the two objects have the same angular diameter.

FIGURE 4

What Is a Light Year?

The fact that Earth is the only habitable planet in this Solar System is well established. There are, however, innumerable other stars besides the Sun, and some of them certainly have planets orbiting them, though we have yet to positively identify one of these stars. The distances to these stars are immense. Their light takes many years to reach us here on Earth. These stars are being studied now, and one of the fundamental facts to be determined is their distance from the Sun. Typical units such as miles and kilometers are awkward to measure such distances; therefore, a unit known as the **light year** is used.

Which number is easier to understand and work with: 5,840 days or 16 years? Both represent the same amount of time. Most people would choose 16 years because smaller numbers are easier to understand. Distances in the Universe are more difficult to comprehend or imagine when they are measured in units such as kilometers or miles. This led scientists to develop a new unit of measurement which makes the astronomical distances more manageable—the light year.

The concept of a light year is sometimes difficult to understand partly because of the words themselves. The term "light year" uses what is normally thought of as a time unit, the year, to measure a distance. But time units are often used to talk about distances. People often talk about how *far* it is to some destination by describing how *long* it takes to get there. As an example, it takes about four hours to fly from the East Coast to the West Coast. Although a time unit is being used, distance is actually being represented.

A light year is defined as the distance that light travels in one Earth year. Light moves extremely fast, 300 thousand km/s. In one second light can travel around Earth almost four times. Nothing travels faster; light is the speed limit. In 31 million seconds—or one year—light will travel a distance of 9.46 trillion kilometers, or 240 million times around Earth. This distance equals one light year, abbreviated "ly."

Distances in the universe are so large that it helps to express them in the scale of light years. Consider the distance to the star Sirius—almost 85 trillion kilometers. That is a huge number to comprehend. Using the light year as the unit of measurement, the distance becomes only 9 ly, much easier to work with. The light year is an appropriate unit to measure vast distances.

The speed of light makes everything appear to happen instantly in our everyday experience. When we watch a soccer game and see someone kick the ball, we assume that the ball was kicked right then, not five minutes before we saw it. For all practical purposes, we are safe in that assumption because light travels so fast. In order for us to see the soccer ball, we must see the light that is being reflected from it, and it does take time for the light to travel from the ball to our eyes. However, the amount of time is far too short to measure. If the distance from the ball to our eyes were 10 m, the light reflecting off the ball would take only 300 millionths of a second to reach our eyes.

Stars are millions and millions of kilometers away. To see a star, that star's light must travel across space to our eyes. The time required for light to travel such a huge distance is easily measured. If the star is 5 ly away, then the light we are seeing from that star took five years to travel to our eyes. It also means that what we see happening at that star is actually what happened five years ago, not what is happening in the star's present. If we see a flare from the star's surface, we are seeing an event that happened five years ago.

Imagine that there is a planet with people on it that is 50 ly away from Earth. These people have an extremely powerful telescope and can actually make out the details of what is happening on Earth. If they aim their telescope at Europe, they will see World War II being fought since it was happening 50 years ago. They will not see the events of 1992 on Earth until the year 2042.

This presents a challenge for the astronomers who study stars. They can never see what is going on in a star's present, only its past. In a sense they are detectives trying to solve a crime without all the clues, and what evidence they do have is years out of date.

Hubble Space Telescope

All our knowledge about the Universe is a result of what we observe, yet with the naked eye, we can see only about 6,000 of the hundred billion stars in our own galaxy, the Milky Way. Our largest ground-based telescopes have extended our vision to reveal a universe with an estimated hundred billion galaxies, each populated by several hundred billion stars.

Radiation in the form of light brings us the information needed to understand the past. Light travels fast, but space is so vast that much time passes before the light from distant objects reaches us. When it is collected by the Hubble Space Telescope this information will tell us about the conditions which prevailed at the source when the light was emitted. So in effect, we are "looking back in time."

The Hubble Space Telescope is the largest astronomical observatory ever placed in orbit. The telescope is in orbit 595 kilometers above Earth, and unlike most observatories, is outside our atmosphere. From orbit, the telescope can detect light before it is absorbed or distorted by the atmosphere. It can "see" stars that release infrared and ultraviolet light that, because of the atmosphere, never reaches telescopes on Earth. The 11,300 kg observatory is about the size of a bus and looks like a tower of stacked silver cannisters. The Hubble Space Telescope uses five instruments to study the Universe: two cameras, two spectrographs, and one photometer. NASA plans to install an infrared detector aboard the Hubble in 1997.

The two cameras record light that is translated into pictures of the Universe. The spectrograph is used to separate radiation by energy. By studying the intensity and distribution of radiation, scientists can determine an object's chemistry, temperature, and density. The photometer records the total light from an object in space and notes any changes in brightness in fractions of a second. Astronomers use the data to determine the relation of stars to each other and their distances from Earth. The Hubble Space Telescope is attempting to answer key questions in astronomy and astrophysics: How do stars and galaxies form and evolve? How big is the Universe? What are quasars and other exotic objects? Do other planets exist?

Reprinted courtesy of NASA.

Scale Measurements

Using parallax and angular diameters are two ways of measuring the distance to and size of objects in the Solar System. The **scale model** is another method of indirect measurement used in astronomy and other Earth sciences as well.

Everyone has seen a model of something: cars, airplanes, buildings, and spacecraft, for example. You can use these models to determine what the measurements would be on the real thing. As long as the measurement of any one part of the real object is known, the rest of the measurements can be determined from the model.

For example, suppose the tire on a scale model car has a diameter of 2 cm, and on the real car the tire measures 60 cm in diameter. This means that 2 cm on the model represents 60 cm on the real car (or, dividing each measurement by 2, then 1 cm on the model represents 30 cm on the real car). This is all that is required to determine all the measurements on the real car from the model. If the model is 20 cm long, then the car must be 20×30 or 600 cm long. If the model is 7.5 cm wide, how wide is the car? If the model is 2.5 cm high, how high is the car?

The same technique can be applied to the Solar System. If a scale model is drawn on a piece of paper, then only one true distance must be found in order to calculate all the others. Johannes Kepler, a German astronomer and mathematician, built a scale model of the Solar System more than 300 years ago.

Each of these methods—parallax, angular diameters, and scale models—is used to determine where Earth is in the Solar System, where the other planets are, and the size of each object. Such information is essential to grasp the significance of the unique aspects of Earth.

If Earth were much closer to the Sun, its oceans—the birthplace of life—would have boiled away long ago. Earth is the only planet in the Solar System with liquid oceans. The plants that came into existence because of the oceans, and the oceans themselves, moderate the amount of carbon dioxide in the atmosphere. Without these, Earth would have developed a runaway greenhouse effect (a topic discussed in greater detail later) increasing the average temperature to hundreds of degrees Celsius. In this sense, it would have been similar to Venus, which is devoid of life.

If Earth had been farther from the Sun, all the water that is in the oceans now would have been frozen, again depriving it of one of the necessities for life, liquid water. Had this happened, Earth would have resembled Mars more closely, another planet found to have no life.

The facts of Earth's location and size are the beginning points to understanding what makes Earth unique and why it is the only planet in the Solar System that sustains life. These facts only become apparent when Earth is placed in the context of the rest of the Solar System. The comparisons which then arise between Earth and the other planets lead to a greater appreciation of our place in the Solar System and Universe.

Scouting Earth/Moon

. . . Soon they [Centaurian explorers] would perceive that the double planet was a fairly small planet attended by an unusually large satellite. Their instruments would reveal the Moon to be an airless, waterless world, its axial rotation captured by its primary, its surface temperatures spanning the range from 240° F to −200° F, its tortured surface preserving the scars of uncounted past events. The planet Earth, in contrast, would seem a beautiful, bright colored sphere. It would be partly veiled by whorls and streaks of white gases in its otherwise semitransparent atmosphere. The colors of the planet would be blue, white, brown, dark green, and russet red. Sometimes, excitingly, a unique bright-silver glitter would shine from the surface.

Instrumental analysis would show that Earth's atmosphere is a combination of nitrogen and oxygen, lightly spiced with carbon dioxide, argon, and trace elements. It is thick enough to serve as a global heat-transfer mechanism and as a shield against lethal energetic particles and bits of rocky solar-system debris racing in at hypersonic velocities. But for all its complex and everchanging white turbulence, the atmosphere would also be frequently semitransparent, giving the planet a window on the universe.

Excerpt reprinted from *This Island Earth*, ed. Oran W. Hicks, (Washington, D.C.: Scientific and Technical Information Division, Office of Technology Utilization, NASA, 1970) p 14, courtesy of NASA.

The Parallax Effect

There are two ways to measure distance, directly and indirectly. When we use a tape measure or a meter stick and measure a distance, we are making a direct measurement. If we look at two chairs across the room, compare their relative sizes, and then infer which chair is closer, we are measuring indirectly. Now consider distances on a much larger scale—like those of the Solar System. Imagine being faced with the task of using ordinary rulers and scales to measure the circumference of Earth or the distance from Earth to Venus. To find out how big the other planets are and how far away they are, we must use forms of indirect measurement. Three common methods are scale measurement, measurement by parallax, and angular diameter.

One of the methods of indirect measurement takes advantage of the **parallax effect**. To demonstrate this phenomenon,

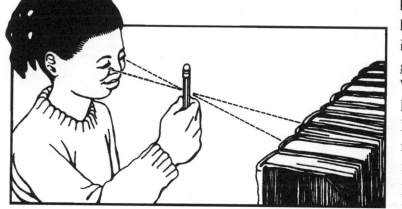

hold a pencil in front of you at arm's length and look at it with one eye. Line it up with something in the background, a clock on the wall or a tree. Without moving the pencil or your head, look at it with your other eye. Notice that the pencil appears to have moved against the background (see figure 1). This apparent change of position against background objects when viewed from different points of observation is called the parallax

FIGURE 1

effect. Each of our eyes is a different point of observation; therefore, we experience a parallax.

Several factors affect parallax. Two major factors are the distance between the observer and the object being observed, and the distance between the two points of observation, called the baseline. The baseline must be known if parallax is to provide a useful measurement of distance. In the example above, the baseline was the distance between your two eyes. The fact that there is a distance between our eyes makes it possible to judge distance by parallax. Our depth perception is dramatically reduced when we use only one eye. A criterion for accurately judging distance by parallax, though, is that the observer must be so far away from the *background* objects that there is no measurable parallax effect for them.

The baseline and the distance to the object affect parallax in opposite ways. As the baseline increases, parallax increases and is more useful for measuring distances. For this reason, larger baselines are always desired. As the distance to the object increases, the parallax *decreases*. Therefore, the farther away an object is, the more difficult it is to measure its parallax and the greater the need to have a large baseline. This phenomena explains why stars all look equidistant to the naked eye.

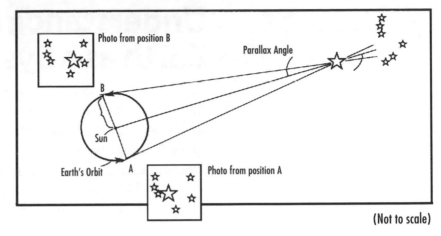

(Not to scale)

FIGURE 2

To measure the distance to some of the closest stars, the required baseline is the diameter of Earth's orbit around the Sun (149,000,000 km), hence the period between the two observations is six months (see figure 2). The actual calculation of the distance to a star uses the *parallax angle* which is one half of the apparent change in its angular position.

Understanding the Earth as a System

We live on a planet of extraordinary complexity; the presence of an atmosphere and oceans with the right chemical composition on a solid planet has supported the development of an abundant diversity of life. Throughout geologic history, the atmosphere, oceans, and land have interacted to produce global environmental change to which life has contributed and adapted. Today, one species of life, humankind, through increasing population and quest for improved quality of human life, has developed the capability of changing our global environment in ways that we are only beginning to perceive, but do not fully understand.

In some cases, such as the depletion of Earth's energy and mineral resources, the effects of human activity are obvious. In other cases, such as the alteration of atmospheric chemical composition, the processes of change are difficult to document, and their consequences harder to foresee. Moreover, the effects of many human-induced changes cannot readily be distinguished from the results of natural change over time periods of decades to centuries.

We know that we have embarked on a global experiment, but we do not know the consequences. Model predictions suggest that the Earth should be warming in response to increasing carbon dioxide and other gases in the atmosphere, but observations are ambiguous. Is the signal lost in the noise of natural climate variability, or are there other processes at work? Until we more completely understand the Earth system, we will not be able to answer such critical questions.

The oceans, atmosphere, and ice-covered regions of the globe are now recognized to be closely coupled in shaping Earth's weather and climate. Both terrestrial and oceanic biota are recognized as exerting a major influence on global climate and the chemical cycles important to life. But the fundamental questions about how the Earth system works remain unanswered.

Over the past 40 years, our view of the solid Earth has been dramatically transformed. The earlier notion of a placid, static globe has been replaced by the dynamism of plate tectonics. Patterns of mountain-building, volcanism, and earthquake activity all fit consistently into this new view.

It is essential that we understand how components of this system interact—from the short time scales of weather systems to millenia of geological time—and how we affect these interactions. Until we have that understanding, we will not be able to predict how human activities will change the environment.

Reprinted from the brochure *EOS: A Mission to Planet Earth* (Washington, D.C.: NASA, 1990) p 3, courtesy of NASA.

After the Warming

Throughout history, the Earth has experienced periods of warming and cooling. Great Ice Ages have alternated with warmer periods, flooding coastlines, perpetuating deserts, and annihilating entire ecosystems. Over the course of human history, rising and falling temperatures have influenced the flourishing or perishing of civilizations. During the Little Ice Age (1500–1850), for example, when temperatures averaged only a few tenths of a degree Celsius cooler than today, Europe documented numerous years of famine and plague. Today, global warming, the rising of the Earth's average temperature, is seen by some scientists as a very real possibility—not millions of years from now but as early as 2050. These scientists are predicting that by that date, a global warming of between 1.5 and 4.5 degrees Celsius (C) will occur. To put these temperatures in perspective, consider that during the 10,000-year era of human civilization, the Earth's average temperature has not been warmer by more than 1 to 2 degrees Celsius than it is today.

An increase of this amount could have devastating effects on some areas of the planet. Melting ice caps and glaciers might cause sea levels to rise, while increased heat might cause severe droughts to occur. For each 1° Celsius of global warming, a 160 kilometer shift poleward in temperature zones may occur. The repercussions from these environmental changes would have profound impact on agriculture, animal husbandry, forestry, recreation, industry, and many other human activities. The phenomenon that is responsible for producing a change in the Earth's temperature is known as the greenhouse effect.

What is the Greenhouse Effect?

The greenhouse effect is the process by which the Earth is warmed by the Sun. Energy from sunlight warms the Earth's surface. Some of this energy is absorbed by the surface, and some is re-radiated into space. Certain gases in the atmosphere trap some of this energy which continues to heat the atmosphere. These greenhouse gases, principally water vapor (which is concentrated near the Earth's surface), carbon dioxide (CO_2), and methane, absorb heat and warm the planet to maintain an average global temperature of 15°C. If not for this warming process, the Earth would be uninhabitable, a virtual frozen wasteland at -15°C.

The greenhouse gases carbon dioxide and methane are released naturally by volcanoes, oceans, plants, and animals. But human industry and agriculture also account for significant production, as well as for two other greenhouse gases, nitrous oxide and chlorofluorocarbons. Carbon dioxide is produced from the combustion of fossil fuels such as coal and oil, and from deforestation by the burning of trees and brush cleared from land. Methane is released from crops, livestock, and garbage. Nitrous oxide is emitted by industry and fertilizers. Chlorofluoro-carbons, or CFC's, come from aerosol spray cans, air condition-ers, refrigerators, plastic foam, and solvents. The accretion of these and other greenhouse gases into the atmosphere through human activity has caused their concentrations to greatly in-crease since the beginning of the Industrial Revolution (1750–1914).

Many scientists worry that continued greenhouse gas increases with correspondingly higher temperatures will threaten the future of life on the planet. However, there could be some potential gains from increased levels of carbon dioxide, including an increase in plant growth and the warming of marginally productive northern regions which could enhance their habitation and stimulate growth of vegetation. Regardless of the impact, most scientist agree on one thing—that global warming will occur. The only questions that remain are "how much?" and "how soon?"

Climatic change refers to long shifts (decades in length) in normal climate. While there have been occasional variations in climate such as heat waves and cold spells, these are considered temporary occurrences, not true climatic changes. When the 1980s recorded four years of the warmest temperatures within the past 110 years, some scientists claimed that this marked the beginning of a period of climatic change; others claimed that it was too soon to tell.

Research conducted by Wallace S. Broecker, professor of geochemistry at Lamont-Doherty Geological Observatory at Columbia University, has been led to an interesting hypothesis regarding how fast climatic change may occur. From his studies of records of pollen grains buried in Greenland ice cap samples, Broecker theorized that climatic change may occur so suddenly and dramatically that people would have no opportunity to anticipate it or adapt to it. Broecker cites a period approximately 10,000 years ago when climate change occurred within a period of one century. Known as the Younger Dryas, this period occurred as a mini-ice age in northwestern Europe, Greenland, and maritime Canada.

The occurrence of any long-term climatic change involves complex natural processes. The greenhouse effect is but one of those processes. Others, like variations in the carbon cycle and oceanic circulation, along with overlapping cycles in the Earth's orbit, tilt, and wobble (Milankovich cycles), combine to affect global climatic changes.

The Role of the Carbon Cycle

As a greenhouse gas, carbon dioxide makes up only .03 percent of the atmosphere's dry weight. Yet it is an essential ingredient for maintaining life on Earth. During the carbon cycle, green plants absorb carbon dioxide from the air. In return, oxygen is given off as a waste product and inhaled by animals and humans. Spring-time is the period of greatest plant growth and carbon dioxide absorption. In the autumn, carbon dioxide is released into the atmosphere as leaves fall and decompose. In addition to land plants, microscopic ocean plants called phytoplankton, are also responsible for absorbing carbon and releasing oxygen. For millions of years, the carbon cycle has helped to regulate the amount of carbon dioxide in the atmosphere. Unfortunately, given the rate at which carbon dioxide is presently being released and the rate of reduction in green plants due to deforestation, the right balance of carbon dioxide in the atmosphere that is needed to help maintain the present global average temperature is becoming more difficult to maintain.

Oceanic Circulation

The oceans maintain a pattern of circulation in which the flow of a deep current of salty water empties from the Pacific into the Atlantic. This is due in part to the nature of water evaporation in the North Atlantic. Surface waters in this region are warmer than those of the North Pacific. Warmer waters will evaporate more, leaving greater amounts of salt to flow through the sea from the Atlantic to the Pacific. It is hypothesized that any alterations in salt distribution caused by the transport of water vapor through the atmosphere from one ocean basin to another will affect climate change. Past climate records taken from ice and sediment cores indicate that climate changes have indeed occurred because of such reorganizations. It is hypothesized that an increase in the atmosphere's greenhouse gases may force yet another reorganization.

The Milankovich Cycles

These cycles refer to the studies of Yugoslavian scientist, Milutin Milankovich (1930), regarding the influence that changes in the Earth's orbit have on glaciation. Three specific aspects of the Earth's orbit comprise the Milankovich cycles: over 100,000 years the Earth's orbit changes shape; over 41,000 years the Earth's tilt on its axis changes; and over 19,000 years the Earth has a wobble cycle.

Researching the Issue

Before the turn of the century, some scientists expressed concern about the extent to which fossil fuel emissions could alter the composition of the Earth's atmosphere. In 1896, Swedish chemist Svante Arrhennius predicted that if carbon dioxide doubled, the Earth's surface would warm by approximately 5° Celsius. Many scientists today concur with that forecast. In 1958, David Keeling and Roger Revelle of the Scripps Institute of Oceanography in La Jolla, California began to record the atmosphere's concentration of carbon dioxide on the summit of Mauna Loa in Hawaii. Regular measurements of carbon dioxide taken since that time have indicated a steady rise in this greenhouse gas from 315 ppm (parts per million) thirty years ago to 351 ppm in 1988. These increases in carbon dioxide concentration have been contributed by human activities. Using the records at Mauna Loa, along with evidence from tree rings (which can depict periods of warming and cooling) and an analysis of air bubbles trapped in polar and glacial ice, scientists have estimated the pre-industrial carbon dioxide level to be around 280 ppm. These statistics indicate that human activity has increased the level of carbon dioxide by approximately 25% since the start of the Industrial Revolution (c. 1750).

An important research tool for modern scientists is the use of computer climate-change models of the global system. Powerful computers can examine interrelationships among many climatic features and mathematically factor in "what-if" scenarios. Given a set of climatic change variables, these computers output models which represents how the planet might look based on the provided data. Such modeling is extremely complex, requiring the adequate representation of feedbacks. Feedbacks are atmospheric and environmental conditions that may have an effect on global warming. In computer modeling, positive feedbacks may hasten the process while negative feedbacks may slow it down.

Examples of feedbacks are the effect that types of clouds, their altitude and brightness have on global warming, the effect that sunlight has on melting ice and snow, and the natural circulation of oceans, the rate at which plants and animals utilize carbon dioxide, and how and where carbon dioxide is deposited in sediments.

Debating the Issue

For the past several years, public concern—and scientific controversy—about the greenhouse effect have been growing. Throughout the 1980s, reputable scientists from all over the world have predicted numerous scenarios, many doomsday in their projections. These predictions are based on steadily increasing measurements of carbon dioxide and other greenhouse gases in the atmosphere, coupled with the increase in population, factories, and farms since about 1800. Many scientists and policy makers alike are deeply concerned about the continued increase of these gases, especially as nations like China and India take further steps towards industrialization.

Other equally reputable scientists have angrily disputed the doomsday predictions, likening the threat of world-wide devastation to a "Chicken Little" scenario. These scientists claim that despite the extensive research to date, too many uncertainties remain regarding the potential for global warming. One of their major concerns is with the use of computer models as definitive evidence of a global warming threat. Their position is that, at present, there is no accurate way to incorporate the effects of atmospheric and oceanic feedbacks into the computer models.

Many climatologists predict that the greatest warming will occur at higher latitudes in the winter. According to computer models, areas within these latitudes are expected to be at least twice the global average temperature increase. However, according to Patrick J. Michaels, associate professor of environmental science with the University of Virginia, there has been no significant warming in the Northern Hemisphere since 1930. In fact, Michaels points out that although carbon dioxide measurements have been increasing, there is little evidence of any average temperature warming.

Tom Karl, a scientist with the National Oceanic and Atmospheric Agency (NOAA), claims that the National Aeronautic and Space Administration's twentieth-century U.S. temperature data, used in congressional testimony on global warming, are warm-measurement biased. He maintains that NASA's measurements over the United States warmed up nearly a degree during this century not due to the greenhouse effect, but rather, to what he calls "artificial" warming, i.e., the trend for cities to grow up around NOAA's weather stations.

While the debate among scientists continues, the public and policy makers are asking a major question, "Can we afford to wait for absolute certainty regarding the timing and extent of the environmental impact of global warming?" Just as the calls for further research continues to be expressed, so do the calls for immediate action.

Reprinted from *After the Warming Teacher's Guide*
(Maryland State Department of Education, ©1990)
p 8–10, by permission of the publisher.

Grand Theme 2: Atmosphere, Oceans, Cryosphere, and Hydrologic Cycle

Global Issues

The central theme will be to establish and understand the structure, dynamics, and chemistry of the ocean, atmosphere, and cryosphere, and their interaction with the solid Earth, including climate, the hydrological cycle, and other biogeochemical cycles.

The Earth is unique in possessing an ocean and living organisms. There are growing realizations that the hydrosphere and biosphere, while constituting tiny fractions of the planet's mass, are crucial in establishing the character of the Earth in several ways.

The ocean, to a visitor from another planet interested in physics, would be most quickly recognized as the controller of water and heat, and the relative sluggishness of its circulation makes it the buffer to the variation of the atmosphere on time scales ranging from days to seasons. It also imposes its own pattern on decadal and longer time scales, as manifest in such phenomena as El Niño. The ocean and the cryosphere also are the main control on solar inputs to climate and weather. On longer time scales—10^2 to 10^6 years—the ocean, glaciers, and their distribution with respect to the land vie with volcanic inputs and solar variations in influencing climate. The relative roles of these different effects are still ill-understood; many observations remain that could improve our insight into these phenomena that are so important to human welfare.

It would be evident to a visitor interested in biology that the ocean would be essential to the development of life. Its margins have offered such stable riches as light, nutrients, perches, and protection from ultraviolet radiation through a reducing atmosphere. As life has evolved, its symbiosis with the ocean has made it a phenomenon covering the Earth's surface, as discussed below.

The influence of the ocean on the behavior of the solid Earth is important as well. It has a major effect on the chemistry of the continental crust through the intermediacy of its sediments. The hydrosphere may be important to island arc volcanism by fluxing magmatic activity in subduction zones. Just how hydrated sediments influence this process of continent-building is not clear, and has been much debated for decades. In addition, the ocean may significantly influence the mechanical behavior of the lithosphere; a relatively small proportion of water can weaken rocks so they are more easily subducted.

The ocean is also the most pervasive connecting medium for global biogeochemical cycles. The magnitudes of most chemical reservoirs and their rates of accumulation are strongly controlled by the ocean, which is significantly older than the ocean basins beneath it.

It has become apparent that the atmosphere, oceans, and the hydrologic cycle cannot be considered in isolation, but rather as a more complete system that includes interactions between the biosphere, solid Earth, and perturbations caused by solar variability and orbital changes. Many of the individual components of the system will have been investigated by 1995, and many of the techniques needed to address the Earth as a planet will have been developed.

Reprinted from *Mission to Planet Earth* (Washington, DC: National Academy Press, 1988) p 62–63, by permission of the publisher.

The Greenhouse Effect

Earth's distance from the Sun has been influential in determining its climate. If Earth were much closer to the Sun, it might resemble Venus. Venus is described as a "hellish" place because the atmosphere filters out most of the visible spectrum of light but red. The second planet from the Sun, located between Mercury and Earth, Venus has an atmosphere that is 96 percent carbon dioxide (CO_2). Earth's atmosphere is only 0.035 percent CO_2. The CO_2 layer on Venus is so thick that it holds in almost all of the heat absorbed from the Sun, allowing little to escape—a phenomenon known as the **greenhouse effect**. As a result, the average temperature on Venus is 457° C, far too hot for any life, as we know it, to exist.

Earth exhibits a slight greenhouse effect too, but obviously not to the degree that Venus does. The greenhouse effect is life-sustaining, up to a point. Without it, the average temperature on Earth would be much lower, perhaps too cold for life to exist. At present, the greenhouse effect here is beneficial, but it may not always be so. The greenhouse effect on Earth is primarily due to water vapor in the atmosphere; however, carbon dioxide also contributes to the effect, and it is this greenhouse gas that is causing the greatest concern at present. Carbon dioxide is a byproduct of many things that we do, primarily the burning of fossil fuels—coal, oil, and gasoline. As more and more CO_2 is added to the atmosphere, the greenhouse effect increases, but it is unclear what the impact on climate will be because of many intervening factors.

Made of glass or translucent plastic, the climate-controlled greenhouse is perfect for nurseries to grow seedling plants and flowers. The glass walls and roof permit the plants to get the most sunlight possible. But the glass also traps heat in the greenhouse. "Greenhouse effect" is the name given to this phenomenon when substances, like glass, permit sunlight to pass through them but do not allow radiant heat to escape. Any time you have gotten into a car that has been sitting in the Sun with the windows rolled up, you have experienced the greenhouse effect.

The greenhouse effect exists because of the nature of light. Some forms of light are visible (like the colors in the rainbow) but others, like radiant heat (also called infrared radiation), are invisible. The greenhouse effect involves both visible and invisible light. The beginning of the process can be explained with a common example.

Paved roads can become extremely hot in the sunlight. Two different kinds of light come into play in heating the pavement. The light from the Sun strikes the pavement in the form of visible light. As the pavement absorbs this light, it heats up and then gives off heat. The temperature of the pavement will continue to rise until the amount of radiant heat (energy released to the environment as heat) given off is equal to the amount of energy absorbed from the sunlight. In direct sunlight, the resulting pavement temperature can be quite high, as anyone crossing an asphalt street barefoot on a summer day can testify.

The same principle operates in the greenhouse effect. The visible light from the Sun passes unimpeded through the glass of a greenhouse and strikes everything: the plants, the tables, the floor. These objects absorb the light and their temperatures increase. The objects then begin to radiate heat in the form of infrared li   er, the glass will not permit the infrared light (he   ugh it and escape, so all the heat stays trapp   .

              le accounts for a tiny percentage of
Ea   s than one percent), it acts like the
gl   sunlight to pass through and
he   ng the resulting radiant heat
fro   of the radiant heat is re-
flec O_2 olecules, heating the lower
atm   y, the CO_2 content is not high enough to
trap   d light, but since the start of the industrial
revolutio O_2 is being produced every day as people burn
coal,   d gas. Earth has natural processes that remove carbon dioxide from the atmosphere—photosynthesis and incorporation into ocean sediments—but they may not keep pace. We are in danger of warming up the planet and that presents serious consequences. Weather patterns could change and cropland could become unsuitable for farming. Melting polar ice caps could cause sea levels to rise and coastlines to flood.

These predictions are based on an assumption that global temperatures will increase. Logically, if the greenhouse effect increases, temperatures should rise globally; however, this global impact is yet to be clearly detected. One explanation is that temperatures are in fact not rising. Another is that measuring temperatures globally is a very difficult task, and erroneous temperature measurements may be incorrect in either direction. They may not indicate global warming that is actually occurring, or they may lead us to believe that temperatures are rising

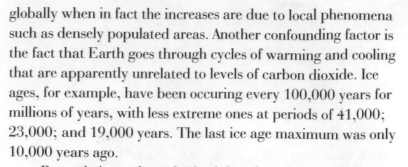

globally when in fact the increases are due to local phenomena such as densely populated areas. Another confounding factor is the fact that Earth goes through cycles of warming and cooling that are apparently unrelated to levels of carbon dioxide. Ice ages, for example, have been occuring every 100,000 years for millions of years, with less extreme ones at periods of 41,000; 23,000; and 19,000 years. The last ice age maximum was only 10,000 years ago.

Recently it was hypothesized that the oceans will serve as a kind of global thermostat to prevent air temperatures from rising above a certain temperature that is not too different from what we now experience. While scientists cannot agree on what the effect of increased atmospheric carbon dioxide will be, almost all agree that there will be some impact.

Grand Theme 4: Interaction of Human Activities with the Natural Environment

Global Issues

Human activities since the beginning of the industrial revolution have increased to such an extent that they must now be regarded as important factors in changing the environment. The effects are approaching a significant stage in altering the concentration of ozone and carbon dioxide in the atmosphere, in changing the surface properties by deforestation and erosion, and in other industrial and agricultural activities. Man is a major force now in the chemistry of the atmosphere and in the allocation of resources on land, and increasingly an influence on the ocean. Moreover, the influence can be subtle, as illustrated by the potential vulnerability of stratospheric ozone.

It has become apparent within the last decade that mankind has the ability to alter ozone, and to thus change the level of harmful ultraviolet radiation penetrating to the ground. We can do so by the direct injection of exhaust gases of high-flying aircraft into the stratosphere, by release of chlorinated gases used as aerosol propellants, as industrial solvents, as working fluids in refrigeration systems, and by complex perturbations to the global nitrogen cycle. These activities lead for the most part to reduction in ozone, but they are offset to some extent by thermal disturbances due to enhanced levels of carbon dioxide, causing a rise in ozone. Assessment of human impact is hampered by lack of understanding of the underlying physical, chemical, and biological influences regulating ozone in the natural state. This matter is critical because the gases responsible for change in ozone—the man-made chlorofluorocarbons and biologically formed nitrous oxide—have lifetimes ranging from 50 to 200 years. The self-cleansing function of the atmosphere proceeds slowly, therefore, and the effects of our actions today will persist for centuries into the future.

Carbon is the largest single waste product of modern society. We have added, by the burning of fossil fuel, over 100 billion tons of carbon to the atmosphere as carbon dioxide since the industrial revolution, with perhaps a quantity of similar magnitude transferred from the biosphere to the atmosphere over this same period as a consequence of land clearance for agriculture. The increase in the burden of atmospheric carbon dioxide is readily detectable. Approximately half of the carbon added to the system remains in the atmosphere and the remainder is presumed to have been taken up by the ocean on its way to the depths of the oceanic abyss, and eventual subduction into the Earth's interior. Attempts to model the process encounter difficulties, however, due in part to deficiencies in our knowledge of the nature of concurrent changes in the global biosphere, interactions with other nutrient cycles—nitrogen, phosphorus, and sulfur, for example—and lack of understanding of the processes of oceanic mixing. The time scales are such as to require a model for the atmosphere, ocean, and biosphere as a coupled system. The matter assumes some urgency since the rising level of carbon dioxide can lead to a change in climate, with associated change in the patterns of rainfall.

The ozone and carbon questions are but two examples of many global issues affecting the environment that must be faced in the years to come. Changes involving soil erosion, loss of soil organic matter, desertification, deforestation, overgrazing, diversion of freshwater resources, and increasing levels of air pollution and acid rain affect the physics, chemistry, and biology of the Earth.

Reprinted from *Mission to Planet Earth* (Washington, D.C.: National Academy Press, 1988) p 69–70, by permission of the publisher.

Reason for the Seasons

The reason why Earth has four seasons—spring, summer, fall, winter—is often misunderstood. In part, this misunderstanding comes from diagrams similar to figure 1 where we try to give you a perspective on a nearly circular orbit as it would appear to a viewer almost in the plane of the orbit. From this perspective, the circular orbit looks elliptical. A similar perspective from directly above Earth's nearly circular orbit around the Sun looks like the diagram in figure 2. Having learned that Earth's orbit is actually an ellipse (although the ellipse is so round it is almost a circle), many people jump to the conclusion that diagrams like figure 1 represent the actual orbit around the Sun rather than a perspective view. This incorrect interpretation of the diagram then causes people to think that the planet is hotter in the summer because Earth is closer to the Sun than in the winter. Consider the following example. At the exact same time it is summer in the United States (the Northern Hemisphere), it is winter in Australia (the Southern Hemisphere). If Earth's distance from the Sun determines the seasons, then it should be the same season everywhere on the planet. In fact, Earth is actually farther away from the Sun during our (the Northern Hemisphere's) summer than it is during our winter.

Earth's orbit around the Sun is more accurately represented by the circle drawn in figure 2. This slightly elliptical orbit does not account for the seasons, but another of Earth's characteristics of motion does.

Earth is spinning. When a ball spins, the line around which the ball turns is called the axis of rotation. Earth's axis of rotation is tilted in relation to the plane of Earth's orbit around the Sun. Figure 3 illustrates the difference. As Earth is spinning, it is also moving around the Sun. The position of Earth in its orbit around the Sun combined with the tilt of the axis of rotation then determines the season. Figures 4 and 5 show how the orbit and axis tilt work together. In the summer the Sun's rays are striking at as close to a 90° angle to the surface as is possible for that location.

Austin, TX is located at latitude 30° and Minneapolis,

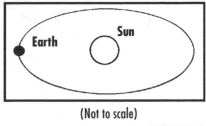

(Not to scale)

FIGURE 1

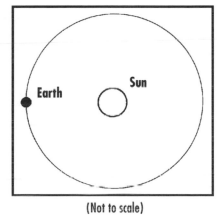

(Not to scale)

FIGURE 2

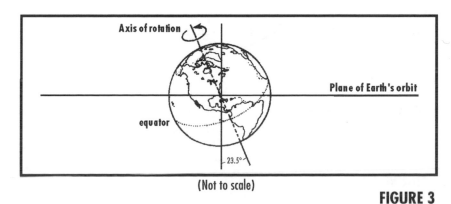

(Not to scale)

FIGURE 3

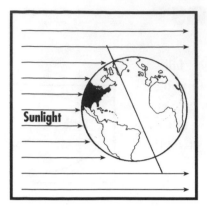

FIGURE 4
Summer in the Northern Hemisphere

FIGURE 5
Winter in the Northern Hemisphere

MN is located at latitude 45°. On the longest day of the year, called the summer solstice, the Sun's rays strike Austin at 83.5° at noon and strike Minneapolis at 68.5°. During this time of year, the Sun's radiation is most intense. Figure 5 shows what happens six months later when Earth is on the other side of the Sun. On the shortest day of the year, the winter solstice, the Sun's rays strike Austin at an angle of 36.5° and strike Minneapolis at an angle of 21.5°. In this case, the Sun's rays are hitting the surface *at a greater slant* than they do during the summer, and the heating is not as efficient. It is not as efficient because the same amount of solar radiation is being spread out over a larger area. Compare figures 4 and 5. The second one represents our winter.

Figure 6 illustrates why perpendicular rays of light are more efficient at heating than slanting rays. In the picture at the top, the paper is standing vertically and the energy from the rays are concentrated in the small area (A_1). But when the paper is tilted back, notice that the same number of light rays, hence the same amount of energy, is now spread over a much larger area (A_2); therefore, it will not heat as fast.

Similarly, when part of the surface of Earth is tilted with respect to the rays of sunlight, it will receive slanting solar rays and not heat as fast. Since Earth is round, some locations can be receiving direct sunlight while others receive it indirectly. This explains why it

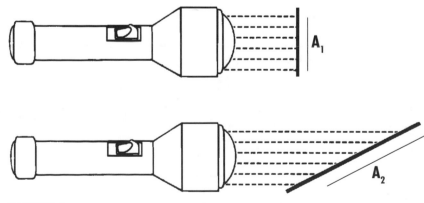

FIGURE 6

can be summer on one part of the planet and winter on another. In addition, because of the axis tilt, the days in summer are longer (allowing more time for solar heating) than in winter.

Phases of the Moon

The Moon is the source of one of the most prevalent misconceptions in astronomy. The misconception is based on the belief that the Moon appears to change shape in a cyclical pattern every 29.5 days.

Throughout recorded history, people have been fascinated with the changing shape of the Moon. Every 29.5 days, the shape of the Moon predictably changes from a complete circle to a half circle to a crescent shape and then vanishes to rebuild again from a sliver of a crescent. Two common misconceptions attempt to explain the changing shape of the Moon. One is that clouds block our view of part of the Moon. The other is that the shadow of Earth falls on the Moon hiding different parts of it at different times. (The only time Earth's shadow falls on the Moon is during a lunar eclipse.)

In fact, the amount of the Moon that is illuminated is constant. We simply cannot see the entire illuminated portion all the time. When we can only see the shadowed ("dark") side of the Moon, it is referred to as the "new" Moon. To understand what is happening when we have a new Moon, imagine yourself in a totally dark room with a ball a couple of meters in front of you. In the dark you would not be able to see the ball. Now imagine that someone is standing in front of you on the other side of the ball and is shining a flashlight toward you. The light would shine on half the ball, but not the half you could see. You still would not be able to see the ball very well because the part facing you is shadowed (see figure 1). This is like the new Moon.

Now if *you* were to hold the light and shine it toward the ball, you would see the half that is illuminated. This is like the full Moon (see figure 2). The illuminated part of the Moon as seen from Earth changes shape between a full moon and new moon because it is orbiting Earth. Figure 3 shows the positions of Earth and the Moon

FIGURE 1   New Moon

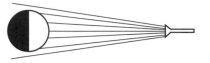

FIGURE 2   Full Moon

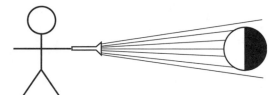

FIGURE 3   The Tilted Plane of the Moon's Orbit

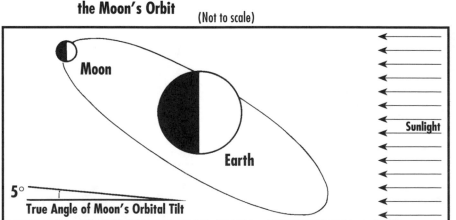

(Not to scale)

Moon

Earth

Sunlight

5°

True Angle of Moon's Orbital Tilt

relative to the incoming sunlight when the Moon is seen as "full" from Earth. Notice that the Moon appears to be above Earth. This is because the orbital plane of the Moon around Earth is tilted with respect to the plane of Earth's orbit around the Sun. If this were not so, there would be a lunar eclipse each month instead of only occasionally.

The shape of the full Moon and the new Moon are easy to explain. The other shapes—crescent, half Moon, gibbous—are more difficult, but each one relates to the path the Moon travels around Earth each month. A model for how these intermediate shapes can be visualized is shown in figure 4. The inner ring of moons shows that half of the Moon is *always* illuminated. The outer ring shows what can actually be seen from Earth.

Earth and Pluto are the only planets in the Solar System with a single moon. Some planets have no moons at all and some, like Jupiter and Saturn have more than one.

FIGURE 4   Phases of the Moon

(Not to scale)

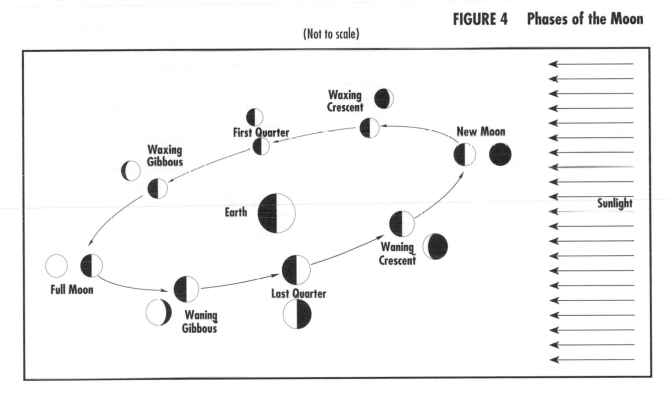

Understanding the Moon Illusion

Over the years many of us undoubtedly have been fascinated by illusions, be they optical or slight of hand. Illusions are fascinating to everyone. One type of optical illusion that is worthy of note to astronomers is the type that employs background objects, lines, or other features to alter the appearance of foreground objects. For instance, two such illustrations are provided here for your amusement and befuddlement (figures 1 and 2). In both cases, straight lines tend to appear bent. If you don't believe that these lines are straight, turn the page on edge and peer down the lines. These are only a few of the many different illusions known.

At times when the full moon is near the horizon it appears noticeably larger than when it is observed higher up in the sky. That this phenomenon is indeed an illusion can be shown by the measurement of the apparent angular size of the Moon under both circumstances. A ruler held at arm's length against the Moon while near the horizon and then higher up in the sky will reveal that the Moon has the same angular diameter. That the Moon's apparent size changes as a function of location is an illusion. This phenomenon is known as the "Moon Illusion."

Of all the attempts to explain the Moon Illusion, only one seems to adequately explain all the known variables. This solution deals with two seemingly divergent points. The first is one of the most memorable of illusions put forward and named after its originator, Mario Ponzo. The second deals with our perception of the sky.

The Ponzo Illusion, more commonly known as the "Railroad Track Illusion," is simply a set of "parallel" tracks that appear to converge in the distance due to perspective (figure 3). Two blocks of exactly the same size are inserted into the field of view. Just as in the preceding two examples, the background influences our perception of the foreground objects—the two blocks. The "nearer" of the two blocks appears smaller than its "more distant" companion. Why is this so?

Since the two blocks both exist in the plane of the paper, distance determination depends upon perspective and not parallax or any other suggestive clues. (We don't know how big the blocks "really" are.) Due to the convergence of the seemingly parallel lines, we accept the narrowing part of the picture as being farther away than the more widely separated portion of the

FIGURE 1

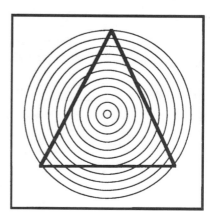

FIGURE 2

tracks. Now, according to the intuitive brain, the top block is
"farther away" than the bottom block. Since the "more distant"
block appears the same angular size as the "closer" block, the
brain accepts the "truth" that the more distant block is "really"
much larger than the nearby block. This is clearly not the case to
the analytical brain, and hence, the illusion. Simply put, the
intuitive brain does not agree with the analytical brain.

You might wonder what the Ponzo Illusion has to do with
the Moon Illusion. The connection seems quite tenuous until you
consider how we perceive the sky. Perhaps you haven't noticed it,
but the "distance" of the sky appears to be a function of where in
the sky we direct our attention. The sky nearer the horizon
appears much more distant than the point directly overhead. The
perception probably results from observing such things as clouds
in the daytime sky. The clouds overhead are nearer; those closer
to the horizon are farther away. If the clouds are "supported" by
the sky, then the sky too must have a similar characteristic.
Suppose you had to estimate the size of the sky as it appears to
you. Remembering the perception of the distances of clouds, you
might say that it is 20 km to the horizon and substantially closer
overhead, for example, 14 km. So a picture of this situation
would resemble figure 4 with you, the observer, covered by the
flattened hemisphere of the sky.

Since we are constantly, subconsciously, subjected to this
perception of the sky, in all likelihood we carry it over into our
perception of the nighttime sky. Figure 5 shows the nighttime
case of this situation. It shows the path of the Moon as an observer would see it. When observing the full moon, in particular,
we see it not as a spherical object, but as a flattened disc. Furthermore, this lunar disc appears to be embedded in the flattened

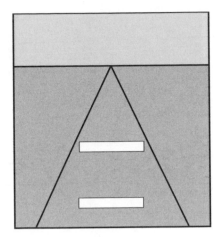

FIGURE 3   Ponzo Illusion

FIGURE 4

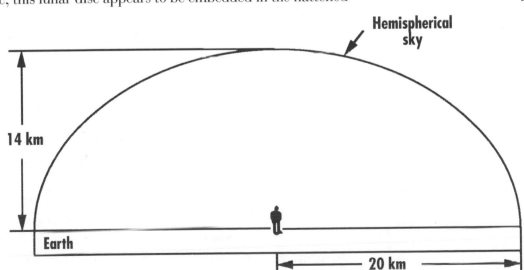

Hemispherical
sky

14 km

Earth

20 km

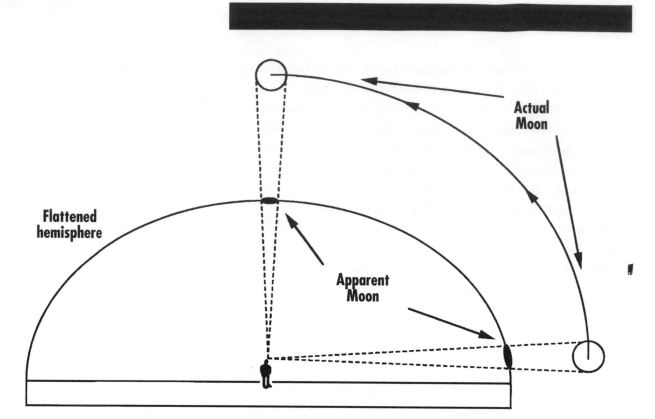

Actual Moon

Flattened hemisphere

Apparent Moon

FIGURE 5

FIGURE 6

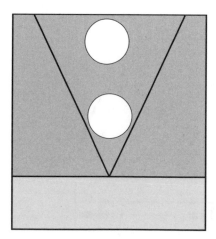

hemispherical surface of the sky. This figure shows how our preconceived notions concerning the sky lead us to conclude that the actual diameter of the lunar disc when close to the horizon is large, and considerably less so when higher up in the sky.

The similarities between the Moon Illusion and the Ponzo Illusion can now be examined. If backgrounds can influence our perception as to the size and nature of foreground objects, it is reasonable to assume that the sky affects the Moon in the same way the converging railroad tracks affect the two blocks of the Ponzo Illusion. If the Moon, like the blocks, has the same angular diameter anywhere in the sky, the apparent size of that body must be directly related to our preconceived notion that the horizon is farther from us than the point directly overhead. The explanation of the Moon Illusion is that it is nothing more than the Ponzo Illusion turned up side down (figure 6).

A few experiments will show that this is a reasonable explanation of the Moon Illusion mystery. It only stands to reason that if the background sky influences our perception of the Moon's size, then anything that "removes" this influence should cause the Moon Illusion to disappear. At the time of moonrise around the next full moon, look for the Moon positioned low along the eastern horizon. It is best to view the Moon from a brightly lit room and through a window dressed with sheer curtains. Draw the sheer curtains aside and look at the Moon. Note its apparent size. Now, pull the sheers across the window. When viewing the Moon through the sheers, the illusion of the Moon's great size disappears. It is through the curtain that you can see the brighter Moon, yet can no longer see the dimmer sky. Evidently, the background sky is part of the Moon Illusion.

An interesting experiment, working with afterimages impressed upon the eye by a bright light, can also show that this foreground/background explanation is correct. Almost everyone is familiar with afterimages. Some evening enter a dimly lit (not dark) room and stare at a bright, unshaded light bulb. Turn off the lamp and watch the afterimages form as you stare off into space. Several afterimages of the lamp will appear because of the almost imperceptible twitching of the eye during the observation of the lamp. All of these afterimages will be the same size by virtue of the fact that they were all produced by the same light bulb.

Note that the afterimages can be made to change size by "projecting" them onto a piece of paper and varying the eye-to-paper distance. As you move the paper toward your eyes, the size of the images shrink. When the paper is moved farther away, the images grow in size. Once again, it is the changing background that affects the perceived size of the observed image. A variation of this activity can be performed outdoors on a starlit night. After forming afterimages by staring at a bright light, project these images to different parts of the sky both high up and low down. You will achieve the same effect as in the darkened room using the piece of paper as your background.

In addition to explaining the Moon Illusion, these activities also explain why the Sun appears much larger when rising and setting. Everyone has seen the "giant" rising and setting sun, but few people seem to note that it too undergoes the same sort of illusory effect. Perhaps this is so because no one can bear to look at the Sun when it is high in the sky and shining brilliantly. The general impression is that the Sun is much larger in apparent size than the Moon. This is not so. The Moon and Sun have almost identical angular diameters. Similarly, our perceptions of the sky also influence our perception of the sizes of bright constellations. For instance, Orion the Hunter, appears much larger when rising and setting than when higher up. Our perception of the sky as a "background" object really can affect the way we perceive the sizes of things in the sky and helps us understand the Moon Illusion.

By Carl J. Wenning, Director
Physics Department Planetarium
Illinois State University
Normal, Illinois 61761–6901

Master Materials List

Originally conceived as a program in leadership development, the purpose of Project Earth Science was to prepare middle school teachers to lead workshops on topics in Earth science. These workshops were designed to help teachers convey the content of Earth science through the use of hands-on activities.

We suggest organizing *Project Earth Science: Astronomy* activities around three key concept areas, explained further in the Introduction on pages 11 and 12. To assist workshop leaders, this Master Materials List includes all of the equipment necessary for using the activities under each Concept Area.

Activities:

It's Only a Paper Moon
Time Traveler
Solar System Scale
Hello, Out There!
How Far to the Star?

Concept Area I

paper plates
metric rulers
index cards
scissors
a watch with second hand or stopwatch
a metric tape measure (30 meters or more)
a calculator (helpful but not necessary)
100 m of string
masking tape
flags (10 per group or student)
marking pens
a piece of candy or other treat per student
construction paper (or manila folder)
chalkboard or large piece of paper
chalk
tape (if manila folders are used)
a single hole punch

Activities:

Solar System Soup: The Formation of the Solar System
The Goldilocks Effect or "This Planet Is Just Right!"
The Greenhouse Effect
Creature Feature

Concept Area II

a bag of vermiculite
containers of water
100 mL graduated cylinder
1000 mL beaker or buckets
stirring rods
a basin
Celsius thermometers
meter sticks
large disposable plastic cups

reflector lamps (with clamp) or gooseneck lamps with
   75-watt bulb
a watch or clock
something to prop up thermometers
rubber bands
Celsius thermometers
a single hole punch
plastic wrap
a large bag of potting soil
graph paper
construction paper
scissors
glue
aluminum foil
straws
toothpicks
paper cups
transparent tape
floral wire

Concept Area III

one or two globes
bright light source (a lamp with at least a 75-watt bulb)
an extension cord
Ping-Pong balls
cardboard
15-cm diameter Styrofoam ball
a pencil
black paint (suitable for Styrofoam)

Activities:

Reason for the Seasons
Ping-Pong Phases

Bibliography

This annotated bibliography was compiled by the staff, consultants, and participants of Project Earth Science at Horizon Research, Inc. of Chapel Hill, North Carolina. It is not a complete representation of resources in astronomy, but will assist teachers in further exploration of this subject.

The entries are subdivided into the following categories:

Activities and Curriculum Projects   This category includes complete curricula, multi-disciplinary units, and collections of hands-on activities. Entries identified as "curriculum" are complete units designed to be used as a series of lessons, while entries noted as "activities" are collections of individual activities.

Books and Booklets   Textbooks, story books, and booklets are included in this category.

Audiovisual Materials   Media materials listed in this section include videotapes, filmstrips, and slides.

Instructional Aids   Included in this category are charts, diagrams, games, models, photographs, and posters.

Information and References   This category lists additional resources such as: bulletins, bibliographies, catalogs, journals, newsletters, packets, books, booklets, periodicals, and reports.

NASA Teacher Resource Center   This category lists the National Aeronautics and Space Administration Resource Centers which serve each state.

Each entry begins with a quick reference formula in brackets, a reference, a brief annotation, and an address. The (quick reference) formula consists of:

Category Type   The specific type of item for the category.
Publication Date   The date of publication.
Grade Level   Elementary (K–5), Middle (6–8), High (9–12) and/or All.

Activities and Curriculum Projects

Activities and Lesson Plans for the Middle School Level
(Activities/1989/Middle) NASA publication (TG-20) is a collection of over 100 activities and lesson plans relating to astronomy and aerospace. (123 pages)

NASA (See NASA Teacher Resource Center List)

Activities and Lesson Plans for the Secondary Level
(Activities/1989/Middle-High) NASA publication (TG-21) is a collection of over 100 activities relating to astronomy and aerospace. (293 pages)

NASA (See NASA Teacher Resource Center List)

Activities in Planetary Geology for Physical and Earth Sciences
(Activities/1990/Middle-High) NASA publication (EP-179) contains activities that deal primarily with planetary geology. Activities may also be used to illustrate terrestrial geology. (175 pages)

Superintendent of Documents
US Government Printing Office
Washington, DC 20402
(202) 783-3238

Adventures Along the Spectrum
(Curriculum/Middle) A teacher's guide to accompany the use of a planetarium program about light and energy. These materials may be used independently of the planetarium program. (15 pages)

Hansen Planetarium
1098 South 200 West
Salt Lake City, UT 84101-3003

Astronomy: Activities and Experiments
(Activities/1983/High) Kelsey, L.J., Hoff, D.B., and Neff, J.S. (1983) *Astronomy: Activities and Experiments*. Dubuque, IA: Kendall/Hunt Publishing Company. Manual for teaching introductory astronomy. Numerous observational astronomy activities are included, as well as activities requiring calculations and graphing. (216 pages)

Kendall/Hunt Publishing
2460 Kerper Boulevard
Dubuque, IA 52001

Daytime Astronomy
(Activities/1971/Elem-Middle) Seager, D. (1971). *Daytime Astronomy*. New York, NY: Webster Division, McGraw-Hill Book Company. Collection of simple daytime astronomy activities. These hands-on activities involve making observations and data collection. (74 pages)

Webster Division
McGraw-Hill Book Company
1221 Avenue of the Americas
New York, NY 10020
(212) 997-2220

GEMS
Lawrence Hall of Science
University of California
Berkeley, CA 94720
(415) 642-7771

Earth, Moon, and Stars
(Activities/1986/Elem-Middle) Sneider, C.I. (1986). *Earth, Moon, and Stars*. Berkeley, CA: Lawrence Hall of Science. Part of the Great Explorations in Math and Science (GEMS) series. These six modules use models and myths to convey introductory astronomical concepts. (59 pages)

Superintendent of Documents
US Government Printing Office
Washington, DC 20402
(202) 783-3238

**Elementary School Aerospace Activities:
A Resource for Teachers**
(Activities/1977/Elem) Kopp, O.W. (1977). *Elementary School Aerospace Activities: A Resource for Teachers*. Washington, DC: US Government Printing Office. NASA publication (EP-147) contains activities on a variety of flight and space exploration topics. (127 pages)

Chicago Review Press, Inc.
814 N. Franklin Street
Chicago, IL 60610

**Exploring the Sky: 100 Projects for
Beginning Astronomers**
(Activities/1989/Middle-High) Moeschl, R. (1989). *Exploring the Sky: 100 Projects for Beginning Astronomers*. Chicago, IL: Chicago Review Press. Includes 100 of Richard Moeschl's favorite astronomy activities. (339 pages)

American Association for the
Advancement of Science
1333 H Street NW
Washington, DC 20005
(202) 326-6446

Ideas in Science: Motion in Space—Comet Halley
(Activities/1985/Middle) Series of eight activities using an astrolabe to measure changes in the position of the Sun, Moon, planets, and stars. All activities aid in the understanding of the motion of Halley's comet. (15 pages)

NASA Lewis Research Center
Mailstop 8-1
21000 Brookpark Road
Cleveland, OH 44135
(212) 433-2016

**Launching a Dream: A Teacher's Guide to a Simulated
Space Shuttle Mission**
(Curriculum/1987/Elem-Middle) Story of a simulated space shuttle mission. This guide chronologically outlines preparation for a mock shuttle mission. It provides detailed documentation of all planning stages.

Superintendent of Documents
US Government Printing Office
Washington, DC 20402
(202) 783-3238

Living in Space—Books I and II
(Activities/1987/Elem) Andrews, S.B. and Kirschebaum, A. (1987). *Living in Space*. Nyack, NY: IRM Corporation. NASA publication (EP-222) gives activities designed by *Science Weekly* for the elementary school and written by NASA. Activities are divided into units: Food, Clothing, Health, Housing, Communication, and Working. (each book, 50 pages)

Out of this World

(Activities/1987/Elem-Middle) Part of the Activities to Integrate Mathematics and Science (AIMS) series. Twenty hands-on activities; classified as to the math/science process skills that are used. (69 pages)

AIMS Education Foundation
PO Box 8120
Fresno, CA 93747
(209) 291-1766

Planetarium Activities for Student Success (PASS)

(Activities/1989/All) This series of activities is written specifically for those who have access to a planetarium. (35–70 pages)

Volume 1: Planetarium Educator's Workshop Guide   Assists in developing educational and entertaining planetarium programs and activities.

Volume 2: Planetarium Activities for Schools   Provides examples of effective planetarium activities for elementary and middle school students.

Volume 3: Resources for Teaching Astronomy and Space Science   Annotated bibliography includes school curricula, books, periodicals, films, videos, slides, planetariums, and telescopes.

Volume 4: A Manual for Using Portable Planetariums   A how-to guide for setting up and using a portable planetarium.

Volume 5: Constellations Tonight   With the aid of star maps and a planetarium students find constellations and can create star-clocks.

Volume 6: Red Planet Mars   Observing Mars through the use of a planetarium and telescope. Activities include students in modeling the Solar System.

Volume 7: Moons of the Solar System   Observing the Moon and examining its common misconceptions.

Volume 8: Colors and Space   Learning about the stars and planets from their colors.

Astronomy Education Program
Lawrence Hall of Science
University of California
Berkeley, CA 94720

Project STAR: Where We Are in Space and Time

(Activities/1989/Middle-High) Twenty-one activities designed to help students learn to develop skills in observation and inquiry. Activities center around two main concepts: cycles; and calculating sizes and distances to planets, stars, and galaxies. (176 pages)

Project STAR
Harvard-Smithsonian Center for Astrophysics
60 Garden Street
Cambridge, MA 02138
(617) 495-9798

Ranger Rick's NatureScope: Astronomy Adventures

(Activities/1989/Elem-Middle) Over 30 activities divided into the following sections: A Look at the Universe, Our Solar System, Our View from Earth, Astronomy Through the Ages, Reaching for the Stars, Crafty Corner. Activities are divided into three levels of appropriateness: K–2, 3–5, and 6–7. (76 pages)

NatureScope
National Wildlife Federation
1400 16th Street NW
Washington, DC 20036-2266
(703) 790-4233

Superintendent of Documents
US Government Printing Office
Washington, DC 20402
(202) 783-3238

Wiley Science Editions
John Wiley & Sons, Inc.
Professional Trade Division
605 Third Avenue
New York, NY 10158-00012

McDonald Educational
McDonald & Co. Ltd.
Greater London House
Hampstead Road
London NW1 7QX

Fearon/Janus Book Publishers
500 Harbor Blvd.
Belmont, CA 94002
(800) 227-2375

North Carolina Museum of Life Science
433 Murray Avenue
PO Box 15190
Durham, NC 27704
(919) 220-5551

Harvard-Smithsonian Center for Astrophysics
60 Garden Street
Cambridge, MA 02138
(617) 495-9798

Seeing in a New Light: Astro-1

(Activities/1990/Middle) NASA publication (EP-274) provides activities developed by NASA based on the Astro-1 Observatory mission. Activities divided into six concepts: Seeing the Colors in Light, Seeing the Invisible, Seeing Waves Everywhere, Seeing Into the Universe, Seeing Through a Filter, Seeing Above the Atmosphere. (58 pages)

Seeing the Sky: 100 Projects, Activities, and Explorations in Astronomy

(Activities/1990/Middle) Schaaf, F. (1990). *Seeing the Sky: 100 Projects, Activities, and Explorations in Astronomy*. New York, NY: John Wiley and Sons, Inc. Describes over 100 simple, inexpensive astronomy projects.

Sky and Space

(Curriculum/1982/Elem) Series of student task cards which explain each activity. Activities are hands-on and require a limited number of materials.

Solar System

(Curriculum/1982/Elem) A workbook designed for below average readers (below a 2.5 grade level). It includes hands-on activities and written exercises.

Spacewalk

(Activities/1990/Middle) A collection of space science activities assembled by Project Space. They include: "Rockets," "Satellites and Orbits," "Exploring the Planets," "The Shuttle," "Space Station," "Life in Space," "Food in Space," "Toys in Space," "Spinoffs," and "Astronauts."

Support Program for Instructional Competency in Astronomy (SPICA)

(Activities/1989/All) A variety of astronomy activities developed by SPICA workshop participants. Each activity is classified as to grade level appropriateness and scientific processes involved.

Books and Booklets

Astronomy Fact Book
(Booklet/1985/Middle-High) Whittingham, R. (1985). *Astronomy Fact Book*. Northbrook, IL: Hubbard Scientific. This short reference booklet introduces basic astronomical theory and describes the physical and orbital features of numerous celestial objects. Telescopes and techniques of observation are also discussed. (46 pages)

Hubbard Scientific Company
3101 Iris Ave.
Boulder, CO 80503
(800) 323-8360

Astronomy: From Copernicus to the Space Telescope
(Book-Hard/1987/Elem-Middle) Lampton, C. (1987). *Astronomy: From Copernicus to the Space Telescope*. New York, NY: Franklin Watts, Inc. Historical sketch of astronomy from the first astronomers to modern space travel. (96 pages)

Franklin Watts Inc.
387 Park Avenue, South
New York, NY 10016
(212) 686-7070

Astronomy Made Simple
(Book-Soft/1976/High) Degani, M.H. (1976). *Astronomy Made Simple*. New York, NY: Bantam Doubleday Dell. This book is a good source of information and useful as a teacher reference. It covers a large range of topics in astronomy including telescope use. (228 pages)

Doubleday
666 Fifth Avenue
New York, NY 10103

Essentials of the Dynamic Universe
(Book-Soft/1990/High-College) Snow, T.P. (1990). *Essentials of the Dynamic Universe*. St. Paul, MN: West Publishing Company. Includes text, learning objectives, suggested readings, sample questions and lists audiovisual aids. (266 pages)

West Publishing Company
50 W. Kellogg Boulevard
PO Box 64526
St. Paul, MN 55164-1003

Hubble Space Telescope
(Booklet/1989/Middle-High) NASA publication (NP-126) gives an overview of the Hubble Space Telescope development and projected use. (71 pages)

Superintendent of Documents
US Government Printing Office
Washington, DC 20402
(202) 783-3238

Is There Life in Outer Space?
(Book-Soft/1984/Elem) Branley, F.M. (1984). *Is There Life in Outer Space?* New York, NY: Harper & Row. A Let's-Read-and-Find-Out book. This story discusses some of the misconceptions about life in outer space. It is written at an elementary reading level. (32 pages)

Harper Collins Publishers
10 East 53rd Street
New York, NY 10022
(212) 207-7513

BIBLIOGRAPHY

Superintendent of Documents
US Government Printing Office
Washington, DC 20402
(202) 783-3238

NASA Spinoff
(Book-Soft/1989/Middle-High) Haggerty, J.J. (1989). *NASA Spinoff*. NASA publication (033-000-01069-9) illustrates the use of NASA technology by industry and the general public. An informative reference book. (136 pages)

Little, Brown and Co.
34 Beacon Street
Boston, MA 02108-1493

The Night Sky Book: An Everyday Guide to Every Night
(Book-Soft/1977/Elem) Jobb, J. (1977). *The Night Sky Book: An Everyday Guide to Every Night*. Boston, MA: Little, Brown and Company. This book contains activities and factual information that could be used on any level. (127 pages)

The Royal Astronomical Society of Canada
136 Dupont Street
Toronto, ON M5R-1V2

The Observer's Handbook
(Book-Soft/Annual/High) Bishop, R.L. (editor). (1990). *Observer's Handbook*. Toronto, ON: University of Toronto Press. An excellent teacher reference and observer's guide. (208 pages)

Harper Collins Publishers
10 East 53rd Street
New York, NY 10022
(212) 207-7513

The Planets in Our Solar System
(Book-Soft/1981/Elem) Branley, F.M. (1981). *The Planets in Our Solar System*. New York, NY: Harper Collins. A Let's-Read-and-Find-Out book. This story introduces the Solar System and its nine planets. It is written at an elementary reading level. (32 pages)

Harper Collins Publishers
10 East 53rd Street
New York, NY 10022
(212) 207-7513

The Sky is Full of Stars
(Book-Soft/1981/Elem) Branley, F.M. (1981). *The Sky is Full of Stars*. New York, NY: Harper Collins. A Let's-Read-and-Find-Out book. This story explains how to view the stars and ways to locate constellations. It is written at an elementary reading level. (34 pages)

Time-Life Books
777 Duke Street
Alexandria, VA 22314
(703) 838-7000

Solar System
(Book-Hard/1987/Middle-High) Frazier, K. (1987). *Solar System*. Alexandria, VA: Time-Life Books. A reference book of photographs, art work, and information. Information and photographs from Voyager, however, are not included. (176 pages)

Harper Collins Publishers
10 East 53rd Street
New York, NY 10022
(212) 207-7513

What the Moon is Like
(Book-Soft/1963/Elem) Branley, F.M. (1963) *What the Moon is Like*, New York, N.Y: Harper Collins. A Let's-Read-and-Find-Out book. This story describes the surface of the Moon. It is written at an elementary reading level. (31 pages)

Audiovisual Materials

The Gaia Hypothesis
(Video/1984/High) Lynn Margulis explores the origin of the Universe and explains the hypothesis that a planet's atmosphere may be used to investigate the possibility of life on the planet. (30 min.)

NASA (See NASA Teacher Resource Center List)

Journey through the Solar System
(Video/1982/Middle-High) The series includes:
The Veil of Venus (Episode 3, 30 min.) This program outlines numerous properties of Venus and shows how it is very different from Earth. It also contains footage from the Pioneer mission.
Life on Mars (Episode 8, Two 15 min. parts) Compares our knowledge of Mars before and after the Viking mission.

NASA (See NASA Teacher Resource Center List)

Living and Working in Space
(Video/1985/Middle) Shows what life is like on the shuttle missions. Contains footage of several experiments on board the shuttle, the repair of a satellite, deployment of satellites, eating, exercising, sleeping, and landing. (30 min.)

NASA (See NASA Teacher Resource Center List)

Portrait of the Earth—The Story of Satellites
(Video/1981/Elem-Middle) Outlines the history of satellites and discusses the different types of satellites and how they are deployed.

NASA (See NASA Teacher Resource Center List)

Private Universe
(Video/1989/Middle-High) Details two very common misconceptions in astronomy by interviewing Harvard graduates and junior high students and showing that their misconceptions are identical. May be purchased or rented. (20 min.)

Pyramid Film and Video
2801 Colorado Boulevard
Santa Monica, CA 90404

The Quest for Contact
(Video/1987/High) Details the work of Search for Extraterrestrial Intelligence (SETI). Features Carl Sagan and other prominent astronomers. (32 min.)

Astronomical Society of the Pacific
390 Ashton Avenue
San Francisco, CA 94112

Shuttle Life in the World of Weightlessness
(Video/1985/Middle) Sally Ride hosts this firsthand look at working, eating, sleeping, exercising, and playing in weightlessness. (30 min.)

NASA (See NASA Teacher Resource Center List)

Corporation for Public Broadcasting
The Annenburg/CPB Project
PO Box 2345
South Burlington, VT 05407-2345
(800) 532-7637

Corporation for Public Broadcasting

The Solar Sea
(Video/1986/Middle-High) Investigates the relationship between Earth and the Sun. (60 min.)

Tales from Other Worlds
(Video/1986/Middle-High) Explores other planets and moons. (60 min.)

Instructional Aids

NASA (See NASA Teacher Resource Center List)

Astrografix
(Software/Middle-High) A collection of programs which include a game, planetary database, and graphics. (Apple—5 discs)

Educational Activities
PO Box 392
Freeport, NY 11520

The Earth Through Space and Time
(Software/1986/Elem-Middle) The program offers a tutorial on the geologic eras. Has information on the Earth, Moon, and Solar System as well as the phases of the Moon and tides. Allows the student to control a tour of the Solar System. (Apple or IBM)

NASA (See NASA Teacher Resource Center List)

Lost in the Universe
(Software/Middle-High) An astronomical guessing game. Using clues, you try to find your dog which is lost somewhere in the universe. There are 15 options for the location which include stars, nebulae, and galaxies. (Apple disk)

Discovery Corner
Lawrence Hall of Science
University of California
Berkeley, CA 94720
(415) 642-1929

Sky Challenger: Guides and Games for Star Gazers
(Chart/1978/Middle) A star wheel is used to show seasonal changes in the stars.

Learning Technologies, Inc.
59 Walden Street
Cambridge, MA 02140-9990
(800) 537-8703

STARLAB
(Model/All) A model planetarium. The STARLAB system consists of an inflatable dome, a projector, projection cylinders and other optional accessories.

Information and References

Astronomical Photographs
(Catalog/Annual/All) Catalog of slides (35 mm) and prints (8 x 10 and 14 x 17) available from negatives obtained at Lick Observatory, University of California.

Lick Observatory OP
University of California
Santa Cruz, CA 95064

Astronomical References
(Booklet/1989/All) List of astronomy references reprinted from the Astronomical Society of the Pacific's magazine, *Mercury*.

Astronomical Society of the Pacific
390 Ashton Avenue
San Francisco, CA 94112

Astronomical Society of the Pacific Brochure
(Booklet/All) For a free illustrated brochure about the ASP's many other programs and publications, send a stamped, self-addressed envelope to the address at right.

Astronomical Society of the Pacific

Astronomical Society of the Pacific Catalog
(Catalog/Annual/All) Catalog items include video tapes, audio tapes, software, observing aids, books, calendars, posters, slide kits, slide sets, and video disks.

Astronomical Society of the Pacific

Astronomical Society of the Pacific Information Packets
(Booklet/All) Series of information packets. Titles include *Interdisciplinary Approaches to Astronomy* (1987), *Learning about Quasars* (1985), *Astrology and Astronomy* (1989), *Black Holes* (1987), *Astronomy as a Hobby* (1988) (Other titles may also be available.)

Astronomical Society of the Pacific

Astronomy and Space Science
(Catalog/Annual/High) Catalog published by MMI Corporation includes planetariums, slides, software, videos, laser disc players, science laser discs, globes, planetarium models, wall murals, and teaching manuals.

MMI Corporation
2950 Wyman Parkway
PO Box 19907
Baltimore, MD 21211
(410) 366-1 222

Careers in Space
(Booklet/Middle-High) An education and career guide for America's space program. Lists career opportunities and the schools by state that provide training in them. (14 pages)

Final Frontier: The Magazine of Space Exploration
2400 Foshay Tower
Minneapolis, MN 55402
(301) 366-1222

Celestial Products
(Catalog/Annual/All) Small catalog of calendars, posters, maps, and wall charts.

Celestial Products, Inc.
10 W. Washington Street
PO Box 801
Middleburg, VA 22117
(703) 687-6881

NASA CORE
Lorain County Joint Vocational School
15181 Route 58 South
Oberlin, OH 44074
(216) 774-1051 ext. 293

NASA CORE Catalog
(Catalog/Annual/All) This catalog lists all materials available at the NASA Central Operation or Resources for Educators (CORE). Includes videotapes, slide programs, computer software, audio cassettes, and filmstrips.

NASA (See NASA Teacher Resource Center List)

NASA Films
(Catalog/Annual/All) A listing of films (8 mm and 16 mm) which can be borrowed from NASA. Films describe various research and development projects at NASA.

Superintendent of Documents
US Government Printing Office
Washington, DC 20402
(202) 783-3238

NASA Information Summaries
(Booklet/Annual/All) NASA publication (PMS-006) lists sources of non-NASA publications and resources, and is offered without recommendation or endorsement from NASA.

Superintendent of Documents
US Government Printing Office

NASA Publications Catalog
(Catalog/Annual/All) NASA publication (PAM-101/7-87) lists all NASA publications.

NASA (See NASA Teacher Resource Center List)

NASA Report to Educators
(Periodical/Quarterly/All)
Report news and information about NASA. Request to be put on the NASA Educator's mailing list.

Astronomy Education Program
Lawrence Hall of Science
University of California
Berkeley, CA 94720

Resources for Teaching Astronomy and Space Science
(Bibliography/1989/Elem-Middle) This bibliography was published jointly by the Lawrence Hall of Science and the New York Hall of Science in Corona, NY. It is Volume 3 of the "Planetarium Activities for Student Success." Resource lists include school curricula, books, periodicals, audiovisual materials, professional organizations, planetariums, and telescopes. (42 pages)

Sky Publishing Corporation
49 Bay State Road
Cambridge, MA 02238-1290
(617) 864-7360

Sky Publications Catalog
(Catalog/Annual/All) Catalog items include a wide range of amateur and educational materials, such as, star atlases, star catalogs, astronomical photos, laboratory exercises, sky calendars, planetary maps, and astronomical books. (31 pages)

National Technical Information Service
Springfield, VA 22161
(703) 487-4650

Space Science in the Twenty-First Century: Imperatives for the Decade 1995 to 2015. Overview (N8915142, 105 pages), Mission to Planet Earth (N8915143, 37 pages (Booklets/1988/All) Policy and planning statements prepared by NASA and the National Research Council.

Software for Aerospace Education

(Catalog/Annual/All) NASA publication (PED-106) reviews prices and rates the appropriateness of software in the following areas: astronomy, aerospace physics, aeronautics, satellites, rocketry, manned space flight. Also includes a section on laser video disks and Spacelink, a 24-hour computer information database developed by NASA to serve teachers and other educators.

Educational Technology Branch
Educational Affairs Division
NASA Headquarters
Washington, DC 20546

Space Shuttle: The Renewed Promise

(Booklet/1989/Middle-Adult) McAleer, N. (1989). *Space Shuttle: The Renewed Promise.* Washington, DC: Government Printing Office. NASA publication (PAM-521) describes the modifications in and the recovery of the Shuttle program from the time of the Challenger accident in 1986. (24 pages)

Superintendent of Documents
US Government Printing Office
Washington, DC 20402
(202) 783-3238

Subject Bibliographies

(Catalog/Annual/All) A listing of NASA publications on a specific subject. (Other topics may also be available.) Sample bibliographies include: Earth Sciences; Educational Publications; Scientific and Technical Publications; Space, Rockets, and Satellites; Weather.

Superintendent of Documents
US Government Printing Office
Washington, DC 20402
(202) 783-3238

The Universe in the Classroom

(Newsletter/Quarterly/All) This astronomy newsletter is available free of charge to teachers, school libraries and administrators. Requests should be made on school letterhead.

Astronomical Society of the Pacific
390 Ashton Avenue
San Francisco, CA 94112

The Universe in Your Desk

(Bibliography/1989/High) A book of resources for teaching astronomy. Lists textbooks, periodicals, reference materials, professional organizations, general readings for teachers, general readings for students, activity and laboratory manuals, observer's guides, maps, atlases, slide sets, audio tapes, films, videotapes, computer software, equipment, telescopes, and instructional aids.

Information and References 17
Project STAR
Center for Astrophysics
60 Garden Street
Cambridge, MA 02138
(617) 495-9798

This Island Earth

(Booklet/1970/All) Accounts in the book emphasize the beauty and uniqueness of Earth among the other planets.

Superintendent of Documents
US Government Printing Office
Washington, DC 20402
(202) 783-3238

NASA Teacher Resource Centers

The NASA Teacher Resource Centers are organized by region. For NASA education materials, contact the Center listed for your state.

Alaska, Arizona, California, Guam, Hawaii, Idaho, Montana, Nevada, Oregon, Utah, Washington, Wyoming

NASA Ames Research Center
Mail Stop TO25
Moffett Field, CA 94035
or
NASA Jet Propulsion Laboratory
(415) 694-3574
(818) 354-6916
Mail Code CS-530
4800 Oak Grove Drive
Pasadena, CA 91103

Florida, Georgia, Puerto Rico, Virgin Islands

NASA Kennedy Space Center
Education Resource Library
Mail Code ERL
JFK Space Center, FL 32899
(407) 867-4090
(407) 867-9383

Illinois, Indiana, Michigan, Minnesota, Ohio, Wisconsin

NASA Lewis Research Center
Mail Stop 8-1
21000 Brookpark Road
Cleveland, OH 44135
(216) 433-2016
(216) 433-2017

Connecticut, District of Columbia, Delaware, Massachusetts, Maryland, Mississippi, New Hampshire, New Jersey, New York, Pennsylvania, Rhode Island, Vermont

NASA Goddard Space Flight Center
Mail Code 130.3
Greenbelt, MD 20771
(301) 286-8570

Colorado, Kansas, North Dakota, Nebraska, New Mexico, Oklahoma, South Dakota, Texas

NASA Johnson Space Center
Mail Code AP-42
Houston, TX 77058
(713) 483-8696

NASA Langley Research Center
Mail Stop 146
Hampton, VA 23665-5225
(804) 864-3296

Kentucky, North Carolina, South
Carolina, Virginia, West Virginia

NASA Space and Rocket Center
Tranquility Base
Huntsville, AL 35807
(205) 544-5812

Alabama, Arkansas, Iowa, Louisiana,
Missouri, Tennessee

NASA Stennis Space Center
Building 1200
Stennis Space Center, MS 39529
(601) 688-3338

Mississippi

NASA Regional Teacher Resource Centers

NASA education materials are also available from the following
centers listed alphabetically by state.

U.S. Space Foundation
1525 Vapor Trail
Colorado Springs, CO 80916
(719) 550-1000

Delaware Teacher Center
Central Middle School
Delaware Avenue
Dover, DE 19901
(302) 736-5569

National Air and Space Museum
Smithsonian Institution
Education Resource Center, P-700
Washington, DC 20560
(202) 786-2109

Parks College
St. Louis University
400 Falling Springs Road
Cahokia, IL 62206
(618) 337-7500

Museum of Science and Industry
57th Street and Lakeshore Drive
Chicago, IL 60637
(312) 684-1414

University of Evansville
School of Education
1800 Lincoln Avenue
Evansville, IN 47714
(812) 479-2393

Kansas Cosmosphere and Space Center
1100 N. Plum Street
Hutchinson, KS 67501
(316) 662-2305

Waterfield Library
Murray State University
Murray, KY 42071
(502) 762-4420

Bossier Parish Community College
2719 Airline Drive
Bossier City, LA 71111
(318) 746-7754

Northern Michigan University
Olson Library Media Center
Marquette, MI 49855
(906) 227-2117

Central Michigan University
Ronan Hall
Mount Pleasant, MI 48859
(517) 774-4387

Mankato State University
P.O. Box 52
Mankato, MN 56001
(507) 389-1516

St. Cloud University
Center for Information Media
St. Cloud, MN 56301
(612) 255-2062

The City College
NAC 5/224
Convent Avenue and 138th Street
New York, NY 10031
(212) 690-6993

J. Murrey Atkins Library
University of North Carolina
Charlotte, NC 28223
(704) 547-2559

Oklahoma State University
300 N. Cordell Street
Stillwater, OK 74078-0422
(405) 744-7015

University of Pittsburgh
823 William Pitt Union
Pittsburgh, PA 15260
(412) 648-7010

Region XVI Education Services Center
Media Services
P.O. Box 306000
Amarillo, TX 79120
(806) 376-5521

University of Wisconsin at LaCrosse
Morris Hall, Room 200
LaCrosse, WI 54601
(608) 785-8650

Discovery World
618 W. Wisconsin Avenue
Milwaukee, WI 53233
(414) 765-9966